STEAM

⊢ Tales ⊢

Alice in Wonderland

Lewis Carroll

Adaptation by Katie Dicker

WELBECK

Published in 2021 by Welbeck Children's Books
An imprint of Welbeck Children's Limited, part of Welbeck Publishing Group
20 Mortimer Street London W1T 3JW

The publishers would like to thank the following sources for their kind permission
to reproduce the pictures in this book.

SHUTTERSTOCK: /Andrey Korshenkov /Venomous Vector.

Every effort has been made to acknowledge correctly and
contact the source and/or copyright holder of each picture,
any unintentional errors or omissions will be corrected in
future editions of this book.

ISBN 978 1 78312 778 8

FSC
MIX
Paper
FSC® C144853

Printed in Dongguan, China

10 9 8 7 6 5 4 3 2 1

Author: Lewis Carroll
Adaptation: Katie Dicker
Illustration: Gustavo Mazali
Text and design: Tall Tree Ltd.
Editorial Manager: Joff Brown
Design Manager: Sam James
Production: Melanie Robertson

Contents

Chapter 1

Down the Rabbit Hole

The warm sun was getting uncomfortable now. Alice yawned and stretched as she sat up by the riverbank. She was getting bored—there was nothing more she could do! Her sister was reading quietly beside her. Alice had taken a few peeks at the book, but it had no pictures or conversations to hold her attention.

"What's the use of a book," thought Alice, "without pictures or conversations?"

Alice was just wondering whether to make a daisy chain (was it worth the effort of getting up to pick some daisies?) when a white rabbit with pink eyes scurried past her. Alice's sister was so engrossed in her book, she didn't seem to notice.

"Oh dear! Oh dear! I shall be too late!" the Rabbit exclaimed, examining a pocket watch he'd taken from his colorful waistcoat. At first Alice thought there was nothing strange about a rabbit running by, but it crossed her mind she'd never seen a rabbit wearing a waistcoat before, let alone one with a watch in his pocket! Alice couldn't help but follow.

"I'm just going to pick some daisies!" she said to her sister, as she leapt up and raced across the field after the curious little creature. She caught sight of the White Rabbit disappearing down a large rabbit hole under the hedge. Without another thought, Alice went down after it, not thinking in the slightest how she would ever get out again.

At first, the rabbit hole seemed like an ordinary dark tunnel, but before Alice knew what was happening it dipped unexpectedly, and she found herself falling down, down, down. She thought it must be a very deep well, or perhaps she was just falling slowly?

It was too dark to see below her, but the sides of the "well" appeared to be covered in cupboards, bookshelves, pictures, and maps. As Alice passed one shelf, she reached out and took a jar. It was labeled "ORANGE MARMALADE," but to her disappointment there was nothing in it. Alice clung tightly to the empty jar, not wanting to drop it and cause harm to anyone below, until she could place it back on a shelf as she fell past.

Down, down, down she continued to fall. Would it never end? "I wonder how many miles I've fallen now?" she thought. "Perhaps I'm traveling to the center of the Earth?"

With all this spare time, Alice thought this might be a good moment to practice her studies. She was just remembering that the center of the Earth was about 4,000 miles down. She kept thinking about her predicament. "I wonder if I'll fall through the whole Earth? And meet people who walk with their heads downward! I'd have to ask them what country I'd gotten to. Australia? New Zealand?" Alice practiced curtseying as she said it (which wasn't at all easy when falling through the air!). Then she considered it might be rude if she didn't know where she was, and she couldn't possibly ask, but perhaps there'd be a sign somewhere to tell her.

✋ LEVITATING PAPER CLIPS

The force of **gravity** keeps Alice falling. Would Alice be able to defy gravity on another object using a magnet? The power of magnetism can even lift heavy metal objects, if it's strong enough.

Turn to page 16 to find out how to defy gravity by making a paper clip levitate, using magnetism.

WHAT IS DOWN?

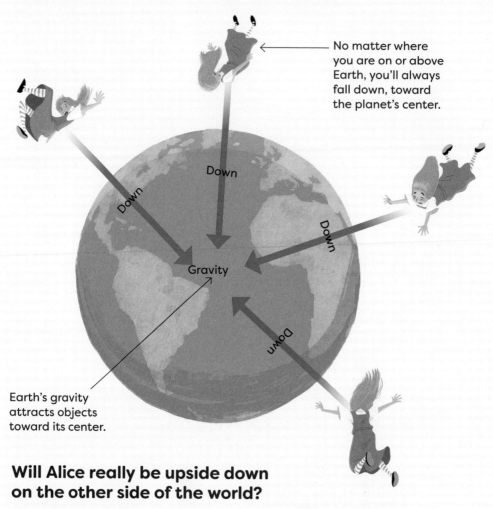

No matter where you are on or above Earth, you'll always fall down, toward the planet's center.

Down

Down

Down

Gravity

Down

Earth's gravity attracts objects toward its center.

Will Alice really be upside down on the other side of the world?

Every object with mass creates gravity and the more mass an object has, the greater its force of gravity. A huge object, such as Earth, has a lot of gravity, which pulls us toward the center of Earth.

Wherever we stand on the planet's surface, the direction toward the planet's center is "down," so if Alice traveled right through the whole planet, she still wouldn't feel like she's upside down.

As she thought and thought about it, Alice began to feel rather sleepy, when suddenly, thump! Thump! She landed on a pile of sticks and dry leaves and at last, the fall was over.

To Alice's surprise, she wasn't hurt in the slightest. She jumped up to explore her surroundings. A passageway lay ahead, and she could just see the White Rabbit hurrying along. Alice followed as quickly as she could.

"Oh, my ears and whiskers, how late it's getting!" the White Rabbit exclaimed. Alice thought she'd almost caught up, when the Rabbit turned a corner and totally disappeared. Alice found herself in a long, low hallway with rows of lamps hanging from the ceiling. There were doors all around the hall. Alice tried each one in turn, but they were all locked.

PARACHUTES

Luckily, Alice landed without being hurt. What could help Alice fall so far but reach the ground gently? A parachute increases the air resistance of a falling object, slowing it down so it lands safely.

Turn to page 14 to find out how to make a parachute so that objects can fall slowly and land gently.

Alice was just wondering how she'd ever get out of the hall again, when she spotted a small glass table in the middle of the room. Lying on the table was a tiny golden key! Alice presumed it must belong to one of the locked doors, but as she tried the key in each of the locks, she found that either the locks were too big or the key was too small. It was no use at all. As Alice surveyed the room for a second time, her arm brushed against a low curtain she hadn't noticed before. When she pulled the curtain to one side, it revealed a tiny door, perhaps 15 inches high. Alice tried the little key in the lock and, to her delight, it clicked open!

The door led to a small passageway, rather like a rat-hole. Alice knelt down to take a peek. At the end of the passageway, she saw the prettiest garden she'd ever seen. "Oh, I wish I could leave this dark hall and walk among those bright, colorful flowers," she thought, "and look at those refreshing fountains!" But Alice couldn't even get her head through the door, and even if she could, there was no way her shoulders would follow!

Alice thought how useful it would be to close oneself up like a telescope. "If only I knew how!" she thought. So many strange things had happened that day, it made Alice feel that anything was possible! It was no use waiting by the little door, so Alice closed it and returned to the table thinking perhaps there'd be another key, or some instructions for closing up like a telescope.

To her surprise, a little bottle sat on the table. "I'm sure that wasn't there before," Alice said to herself. The bottle had a label around its neck with the words "DRINK ME" written in beautiful ink. Alice was no fool. She knew the dangers of drinking unknown liquids and wasn't going to drink the bottle just because it said she should! She checked to see if the bottle was marked "poison" or had other clues to its contents. There was nothing to be found, so Alice took the tiniest sip, and found it to be very pleasant. In fact, the drink tasted like cherry tart, pineapple, custard, roast turkey, toffee, hot-buttered toast, and beans. What a combination! Before Alice knew it, she'd finished the bottle in one gulp.

"What a curious feeling," Alice exclaimed. To her surprise, she'd shrunk to about ten inches tall. It was as if her wish had been granted—she was now the right size for the door! Alice hesitated a little, just in case there was more shrinking to come. "Imagine if I shrunk so much, I might go out like a little candle!"

When nothing else happened, Alice made for the door. But to her dismay the door was locked again, and she'd forgotten the key, which lay on the table that now towered above her.

Drink me

Alice could see the key quite clearly through the glass, but there was no way to reach it. She tried climbing up one of the table legs, but it was too slippery. Before long, she was so tired with trying and so exasperated, that she threw herself down where she was and burst into tears.

Alice tried to pull herself together. "Come on, there's no use crying!" she said to herself brusquely, rubbing away angry tears. "You should stop this minute." She often scolded herself like this, but it wasn't always easy to follow her own advice. Sometimes, Alice pretended to be two people at once. She'd even boxed her own ears once for cheating, when playing croquet against herself. "It's no use pretending to be two people now," thought Alice. "There's hardly enough of me left to make one person!"

Just at that moment, Alice's eyes fell on a little glass box lying under the table. "How strange," she thought, "that things keep appearing!" When she opened the box, she found a very small cake inside. It had the words "EAT ME" marked out beautifully in currants. Alice was feeling a little indignant now. "Well, I'll eat it!" she exclaimed. "I have nothing to lose. If I grow larger, I'll be able to reach the key and if I grow smaller, I can creep under the door! Either way I should be able to get into the garden, and I don't care which it is!"

ROUGH AND SMOOTH

Very little friction

Smooth surfaces produce little friction when they rub against each other.

Lots of friction

Rough surfaces produce lots of friction when they rub against each other.

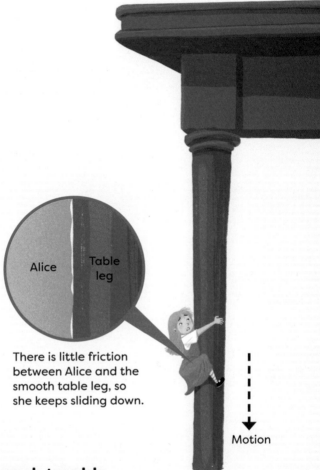

Alice   Table leg

There is little friction between Alice and the smooth table leg, so she keeps sliding down.

Motion

Why does Alice have so much trouble climbing the table leg?

Friction causes moving objects to slow down as they slide past each other. The amount of friction depends on the materials —glass causes very little friction because its surface is smooth, whereas rougher materials like tree bark cause more friction. Alice cannot climb the table leg because its surface is smooth and does not produce enough friction for her to grip and climb.

MAKE A PARACHUTE

See how you can increase air resistance to slow down falling objects and bring them safely to the ground.

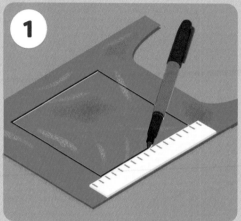

1

Using the ruler and felt-tip pen, draw a square measuring about 8 inches (20 cm) across onto the plastic bag and cut it out.

YOU WILL NEED:
- Ruler
- Felt-tip pen
- Plastic bag
- String
- Scissors
- Tape
- Small toy figure

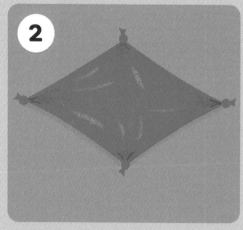

2

Tie a knot in each corner of this square.

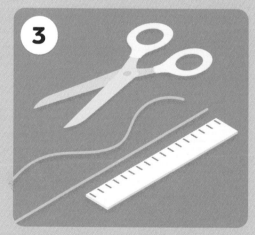

3

Measure and cut two pieces of string that are about 16 inches (40 cm) long.

TIP
Tie the string behind the knots in the plastic square so the string doesn't slip off.

4

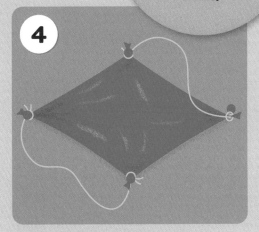

Tie the ends of each piece of string to the corners of the plastic square so they each form a loop.

5

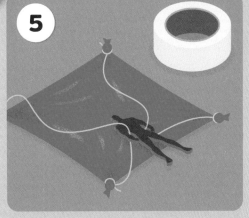

Loop the string under the arms of your small toy figure and hold the string in place with some tape.

6

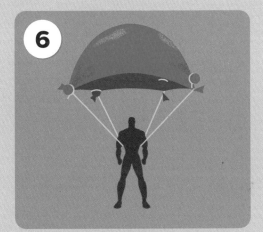

Hold the parachute up high and drop it—watch as the toy drifts to the floor.

WHY IT WORKS

While gravity causes the toy to fall to the floor, the parachute slows its fall because it increases resistance with the air as it moves through it.

LEVITATING PAPER CLIPS

Discover how to make a paper clip levitate—just like magic! Is it possible to make more than one paper clip float at once?

1

Build a simple bridge out of LEGO® blocks which has enough space underneath the deck for your paper clip to float.

YOU WILL NEED:

- LEGO® blocks
- Strong magnet
- Tape
- 3 or more paper clips
- Thin thread

2

Tape the magnet to the underside of the deck of the bridge using the tape.

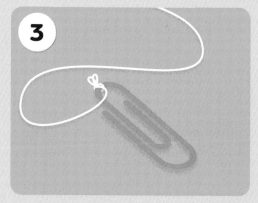

3

Measure a length of thread that is a little longer than the height of the bridge. Tie one end of the thread to the paper clip.

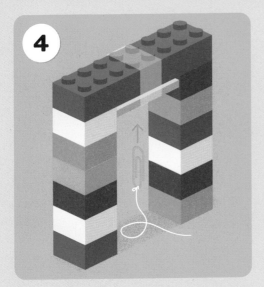

4

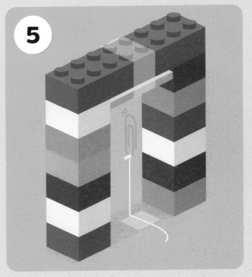

5

Starting from the ground, slowly raise the paper clip up toward the magnet until you feel the pull of the magnet above. Can you suspend the magnet in mid-air?

Once the magnet is levitating, tape the other end of the thread to the surface below.

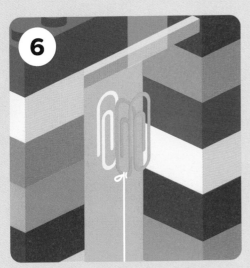

6

WHY IT WORKS

There are two forces acting on the paper clip as it is suspended in mid-air: magnetism and gravity. The force acting on the paper clip from the magnet above pulls the paper clip toward it. At the same time, gravity pulls the paper clip down toward the ground. The point at which the paper clip levitates is where these two forces are balanced.

Can you make more than one paper clip levitate at once? Lightly touch more paper clips to the suspended paper clip, one by one, and see how many will stay.

Chapter 2

The Pool of Tears

Alice ate a little bit of the cake, anxious to know what the outcome would be. She put her hand on top of her head to feel if she was growing or shrinking. In fact, she remained the same size! To be fair, that's what usually happens when you eat cake, but Alice's day had been so full of surprises, she was sure something was going to happen. It seemed very dull that nothing was happening at all. So, she set to work and ate the cake as quickly as possible.

"How curious!" Alice exclaimed. "Now I'm opening out like the largest telescope ever! Goodbye feet!" she cried, for her feet were almost out of sight, they were so far away. "Oh dear, my poor feet, who will put on your shoes and socks now? I certainly can't!" Alice chuckled. It was becoming quite comical. "But I must be kind to my feet," she thought. "They might not walk the way I want them to otherwise! Let's think. Perhaps I could get them a new pair of boots every Christmas." Alice began working out the logistics of this. "How funny," she thought. "I'll have to post them. And how strange the directions will be!"

Alice's Right Foot
Hearth rug
By the fire
(sent with Alice's love)

"Oh dear, now I'm talking nonsense!" Alice giggled. Just then, her head bumped against the ceiling of the hall. In fact, she was now more than nine feet tall. Without further ado, she grabbed the golden key and made for the door.

✋ ## HOW TALL IS A PAPER PLATE?

Alice finds that she is growing taller, as she suspected.

Is it possible to make an object taller without adding anything new to it? It all depends on how that object is arranged in the space around it.

Can you make a paper plate grow taller using just a pair of scissors? Turn to page 28 to work out how to make a plate stretch as high as possible.

Poor Alice. In her haste, she'd quite forgotten there was no way she'd fit through the tiny entrance to the garden. She lay on the floor looking helplessly through the door with one eye. She pulled herself up to a sitting position and began to cry again.

"You ought to be ashamed of yourself!" Alice scolded herself once more. "A grown girl like you, carrying on in this way. Stop this instant, I tell you!" But she kept on crying all the same, shedding gallons of tears until there was a large pool all around her. It was about four inches deep and reached halfway down the hall.

After a while, Alice heard a little pattering of feet in the distance. She quickly dried her eyes and tried to compose herself, to see what (or who) was coming. It was the White Rabbit scurrying toward the hall! This time he was splendidly dressed, with a pair of white leather gloves in one hand and a large fan in the other. He was approaching at speed, muttering to himself as he trotted along, "Oh! The Duchess, the Duchess! Oh! Won't she be cross if I've kept her waiting!"

Alice felt so sorry for herself that she was willing to ask for anyone's help. When the Rabbit came near, she began in a low, timid voice, "If you please, sir..." The Rabbit was startled! He dropped his fan and white gloves, scurrying off into the darkness as fast as his legs would carry him.

HOW SALTY ARE TEARS?

Alice can't stop crying, filling the hall with salty tears.

Depending on what makes you cry, tears contain different levels of salt. **Basal tears** keep our eyes healthy and wet, and contain around 1 percent salt. **Reflex tears**, which wash away dirt and other irritating substances, contain the same amount. Tears that are triggered by strong emotions, like Alice's, are called **emotional tears**. They have slightly less salt in them, and instead contain other substances that can relieve pain and help us feel better. So Alice's tears may not be quite as salty as she thinks!

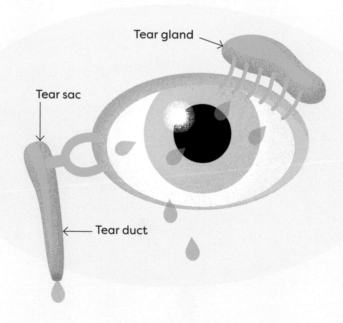

Tear gland

Tear sac

Tear duct

"Oh dear!" Alice picked up the fan and gloves. The hall was getting very hot now and she was glad of the fan to cool herself. "How strange everything is today! And yesterday everything was so normal. Perhaps I've changed overnight? Let me think, was I the same when I got up this morning? I do, perhaps, remember feeling a little different. But if I'm not the same, then who am I?" Alice began to think of all the children she knew of her own age to see if she might have become one of them.

"I can't be Ada, because her hair is in ringlets, and I can't be Mabel because I know more facts than her," Alice thought. "I wonder if I can remember all the things I used to know? Let me see… four times five is twelve, and four times six is thirteen, and four times seven is… Oh dear! I'm not getting anywhere. Let's try geography. London is the capital of Paris, and Paris is the capital of Rome, and Rome… no, no, that's all wrong, I'm certain! Perhaps I've been changed for Mabel!"

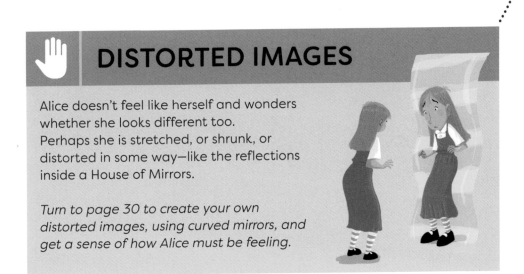

✋ DISTORTED IMAGES

Alice doesn't feel like herself and wonders whether she looks different too.
Perhaps she is stretched, or shrunk, or distorted in some way—like the reflections inside a House of Mirrors.

Turn to page 30 to create your own distorted images, using curved mirrors, and get a sense of how Alice must be feeling.

Alice kept trying to recall facts she'd learned at school. She tried to recite a poem, but her voice sounded hoarse and strange, and the words didn't come out right at all! "Oh dear!" Alice burst into tears again. "I do wish someone would come to my rescue—I'm getting very tired of being here all alone."

At that, Alice looked down at her hands and was surprised to see she'd put on one of the Rabbit's white leather gloves. "How did I manage that? I must be shrinking again!" Alice went to measure herself against the table and found she was now about two feet high and shrinking fast. Alice soon realized the cause of this was the fan she was using. She dropped it hastily, just in time to stop shrinking away altogether.

"That was a narrow escape!" Alice said, feeling rather frightened at the sudden change, but glad to know she was still alive. "Now I must get to the garden!" Alice ran at full speed toward the little door. But to her dismay, it was locked again, and the golden key was lying on the glass table once more. "This is worse than ever!" Alice sobbed, as she cried more tears. And before she knew it, her foot slipped. Splash! She was up to her chin in the salt water of her tears.

At first, Alice thought she must have fallen into the sea. But she soon realized she was swimming in her own pool of tears. "I wish I hadn't cried so much!" she thought as she swam about trying to find her way out. "I suppose drowning in my own tears is punishment for being a cry baby. I wouldn't put it past this strange day I'm having."

Just then, she heard something splashing about in the pool a little way off. At first, she thought it might be a walrus or a hippopotamus, but then she remembered how small she was, and realized it was only a mouse that had slipped in like herself.

"Would it be any use to speak to the mouse?" Alice thought. "Everything is so strange down here, the mouse can probably talk. I guess there's no harm trying." And so she began… "Oh Mouse, do you know the way out of this pool? I'm very tired of swimming now. Oh Mouse!" Alice presumed this was the best way to approach the little fellow. The Mouse looked at her rather inquisitively and seemed to wink with one of his little eyes but said nothing.

"Perhaps it doesn't understand English?" Alice thought. "It could be a French mouse who came over with William the Conqueror!" With her limited knowledge of history, Alice didn't know the Normans invaded over 900 years ago. She tried again, "Où est ma chatte?" This was the first sentence in her French book. The Mouse suddenly leapt out of the water, shaking with fear. "Oh, I'm so sorry!" Alice cried, worried that she'd hurt the poor animal's feelings. "I quite forgot that mice don't like cats."

"Not like cats?" the Mouse cried in a shrill voice. "Would you like cats if you were me?"

"I guess not," Alice replied. "Although I do wish I could show you our cat Dinah. I think you'd like cats if you met her." Alice went on, half to herself, as she swam lazily about in the pool. "She sits purring so nicely by the fire, licking her paws and washing her face. She's great at catching mice! Oh … I'm so sorry." This time the Mouse was shaking all over, and Alice felt certain he must be really offended. "We won't talk about her anymore if you'd rather not."

"We indeed!" the Mouse shuddered. "As if I would talk about such things!"

Alice quickly changed the subject. "Are you fond of … dogs?" she asked. The Mouse didn't answer, so Alice went on again. "There's such a nice dog near our house! A little bright-eyed terrier. It belongs to a farmer. He says it kills all the rats and … oh dear! I have offended you again!" The Mouse was swimming away as fast as he could, making quite a commotion.

Alice called to it softly "Oh Mouse! Do come back. We won't talk about cats or dogs either, if you don't like them!" When the Mouse heard this, he turned around and swam slowly back to her. His face was very pale and his voice trembled. "Let us swim to the shore, then I'll tell you why I hate cats and dogs."

It was definitely time to go. The pool was getting quite crowded now with all the birds and animals that had fallen into it. There was a Duck and a Dodo, a Parrot and a young Eagle, and several other curious creatures. Alice led the way, and the whole party swam to the shore.

WHY DON'T MICE LIKE CATS?

Dinah would likely see the Mouse as a tasty morsel to eat. In fact, cats in the wild rely on mice and other small animals for energy and wouldn't survive without eating them. This is all part of a natural food chain.

• Every food chain starts with a plant, known as a producer, which gets its energy from the Sun.

• Animals that eat plants, and cannot make their own food, are called consumers.

• Animals that eat other animals are called predators (or secondary consumers). The cat is at the top of this food chain.

Are there any animals that Alice's cat might be afraid of?

Sun

Cat

Plants

Mouse

STRETCHING PAPER PLATES

Can you stretch a paper plate to make it as tall as Alice? Draw and cut out different designs to see how far your plates can stretch...

1

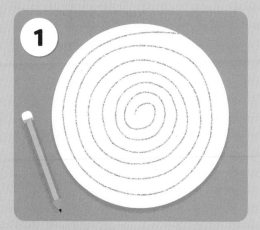

Sketch your design on a paper plate—would a spiral, zigzag or other shape work best?

YOU WILL NEED:

- Pencil
- 3 or more paper plates
- Scissors
- Tape measure
- Paper to record measurements

2

With an adult's help, carefully use scissors to cut out your shape.

3

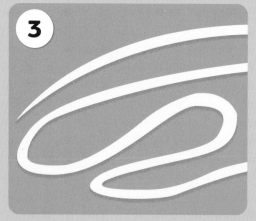

Unfurl your plate and stretch it out—how far can it reach?

TIP

Experiment with how thin you can draw your design. Does this help it stretch farther?

4

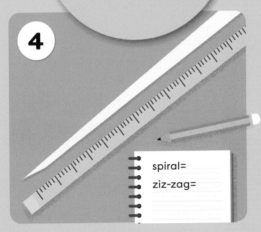

spiral=
ziz-zag=

Use the tape measure to measure the length of your plate from one end to the other. Write down the result.

5

Is there a different shape that would work better? Sketch it out on another paper plate.

6

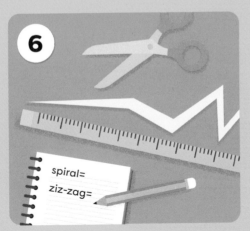

spiral=
ziz-zag=

Repeat steps 1-4, testing out different shapes and patterns, and see which one will stretch the farthest.

WHY IT WORKS

Like most plates, paper plates are shaped as circles. As circles, they take up the least possible amount of space on a table. When you cut the circle into different shapes, its area (the space inside it) can be rearranged to take up more space.

29

DISTORTED IMAGES

A mirror is a smooth surface that reflects light in an ordered way. Try bending a mirror to change the reflections you see.

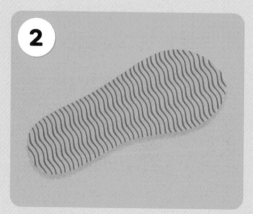

1

To make a bendable mirror, cut a rectangle of mirroring paper (or foil) big enough to cover one side of the flip-flop sole (or cardstock).

YOU WILL NEED:

- Scissors
- Mirroring paper/aluminum foil
- Old flip-flop (or piece of thick flexible cardstock)
- 2 toothpicks/skewers
- Glue (optional)
- Small colorful figurines or board game pieces

2

Lay the flip-flop on the table lengthways, sole side up.

3

Place the rectangle of mirroring paper on top with the mirroring side facing up.

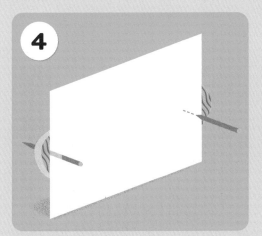

With an adult's help, pierce one toothpick through the mirroring paper and the flip-flop, about an inch from the left edge. Do the same with the second toothpick about an inch from the right edge. If needed, use glue to keep the mirroring paper in place.

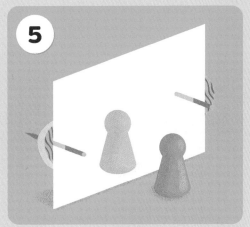

Turn the bendable mirror on its side so that it faces you and place the colorful objects in front of the mirror one by one. Can you see their reflections?

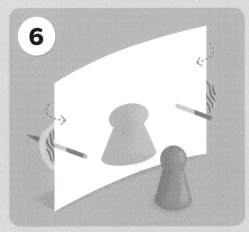

Bend the center of the mirror away from you to make it concave. How does the reflection change? Bulge the center of the mirror toward you to make it convex. How do the reflections differ?

WHY IT WORKS

A flat, smooth mirror will reflect light back to your eyes in an ordered way. This creates a "mirror image" that is true to life. If a mirror's surface is curved, the light is reflected at different angles, creating a distorted image.

Chapter 3

The Caucus Race

When they reached the bank, they were a very strange looking party. The birds had bedraggled feathers, the animals' fur was clinging to them, and they were all dripping wet, cross, and uncomfortable.

Their first priority was to get dry again, but how to do it? As they discussed the matter, Alice found herself talking to the creatures as if she'd known them all her life. In fact, she had quite an argument with the Parrot, who finally said in a sulky voice, "I'm older than you, and must know better". Alice refused to believe this until she knew the Parrot's age, but he wouldn't tell her so there was nothing more to be said.

At last, the Mouse seemed to be taking charge. "Sit down all of you and listen! I'll soon make you dry enough." They all sat in a circle with the Mouse in the middle. Alice kept her eyes fixed on the Mouse. She felt certain she'd catch a cold if she didn't get dry very soon.

"Ahem, are you all ready?" the Mouse said with an air of importance. "This is the driest thing I know. Silence please! 'William the Conqueror had the support of the Pope and was soon backed by the English (who wanted a strong leader after some tiresome years of change at the top). Edwin and Morcar, the earls of Mercia and Northumbria...'"

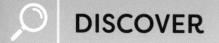
WATER OFF A DUCK'S BACK

Water running off duck's feathers

Oil-producing (preen) gland

Why is it that some creatures, like Alice and the Mouse, can get soaking wet and others, such as ducks, dry off almost immediately?

Ducks and many other birds have a special method for waterproofing their feathers, making water roll right off them! When they wash their feathers (called "preening"), birds use their beaks to pick up oil from an oil-producing gland at the top of their tails (the preen gland). They rub this oil over their feathers to create a waxy coating that stops water from soaking into their feathers. So, unlike Alice and the other animals, a duck would emerge from the pool feeling nice and dry.

"Ugh!" said the Parrot with a shudder.

"Excuse me?" said the Mouse. "Did you speak?"

"No, certainly not!" said the Parrot quickly.

"Ah, I thought you did," said the Mouse. "I'll continue. 'Edwin and Morcar, the earls of Mercia and Northumbria, supported him, and even the Archbishop of Canterbury found it advisable…'"

"Found what advisable?" asked the Duck.

"Found 'it'," the Mouse replied rather crossly. He took no notice and went on, "found it advisable to go with Edgar Atheling to meet William and offer him the crown…' How are you doing my dear?" said the Mouse, turning to Alice.

"Still wet," Alice replied sadly. "It doesn't seem to dry me at all."

"In that case," the Dodo interrupted. "I think we should find a more energetic solution. I think the best thing to get us dry would be a Caucus Race."

"What's a Caucus Race?" Alice piped up, when there was a long pause and no one else seemed willing to say anything.

"The best way to explain it is for us all to do it!" the Dodo replied. First, he marked out a circular racecourse (although he said the exact shape didn't matter). Then he invited all the party to stand along the course, here and there.

There was no starting call. They began to run in random directions when they liked, and stop when they liked, so it was difficult to know when the race was over. But after half an hour or so, when they were all quite dry again, the Dodo suddenly cried out "The race is over!" and they all crowded around, panting, and asking "Who won?"

The Dodo didn't know the answer to this and sat for a while with his finger pressed against his forehead, while everyone waited in silence.

At last, the Dodo said, "Everybody has won, and everybody should get a prize!"

"But who will give the prizes?" a chorus of voices asked.

"Why, she of course," said the Dodo, pointing at Alice. The whole party crowded around her at once, shouting "Prizes! Prizes!"

THE WATER CYCLE

Alice and the animals are dry at last, so where did all the water go? It's as if it has vanished into thin air. But water doesn't just disappear, it evaporates, turning into water vapor in the air. Could they have tried different ways to get dry faster?

Turn to page 42 to make a miniature water cycle and watch the process of evaporation in action.

WHERE DID THE WATER GO?

After half an hour or so of racing around, Alice and the animals are no longer wet.

The water in their clothes (and fur) has been changed from a liquid into a gas in a process called evaporation. Heating water up encourages it to evaporate faster as the water molecules gain enough energy to separate from the liquid. This process can also be reversed, with water vapor turning back into liquid water (condensing) when it cools down. Alice and the animals dry faster as they run around, because the energy from their bodies heats the water in their clothes, encouraging it to evaporate away.

Evaporation (water vapor)

Heat energy from body

Wet clothes

Alice had no idea what to do. In her despair, she put her hand in her pocket where she found a box of dried fruit, nuts, and seeds coated in sugar (fortunately the salt water hadn't got to them). She handed them out as prizes—there was exactly one each to go around.

"But she must have a prize herself, you know," said the Mouse.

"Of course," said the Dodo. "What else have you got in your pocket?" he said, turning to Alice.

"Only a thimble," Alice replied sadly.

"Hand it over here," the Dodo said.

They all crowded around her once more, while the Dodo presented Alice with the thimble and they all cheered. Alice thought the whole thing was very strange, but they all looked at her so solemnly that she didn't dare laugh. As she couldn't think of anything to say, she just bowed, and took the thimble as solemnly as she could.

The next thing to do was eat the treats. This caused some noise and confusion as the large birds complained they couldn't taste theirs, and the small ones choked and had to be patted on the back. But once it was over, they sat down in a circle again and begged the Mouse to tell them something else.

"You promised to tell me why you hate—C and D," Alice whispered, afraid that he would be offended again if she said "cats and dogs".

"Mine is a long and sad tale!" said the Mouse, sighing.

"It's a long tail, certainly," said Alice as she looked in wonder at the Mouse's tail, "but why do you call it sad?" She kept on puzzling about this while the Mouse was speaking, imagining his words written down in a long, wiggly "tail-shaped" line.

"You're not listening!" the Mouse said to Alice severely. "What are you thinking of?"

"I'm so sorry," Alice replied humbly, "you'd just got to the fifth bend of your tail, I think?"

"I had not!" cried the Mouse angrily. "A knot?" said Alice, always wanting to help. "Do let me help you undo it!"

The Mouse only growled in reply.

✋ WRITING PICTURES

Could you create something similar out of words on paper?

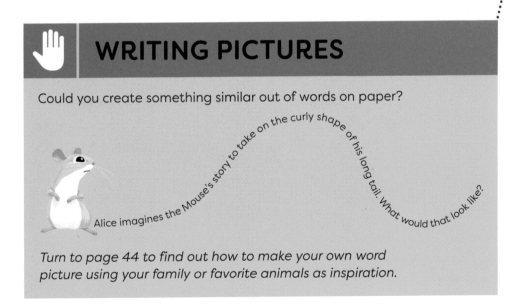

Alice imagines the Mouse's story to take on the curly shape of his long tail. What would that look like?

Turn to page 44 to find out how to make your own word picture using your family or favorite animals as inspiration.

"Please come back and finish your story!" Alice called, but the Mouse only shook his head impatiently and quickened his step.

"I wish Dinah was here," said Alice aloud to no one in particular.

"And who's Dinah if I may ask?" said the Parrot.

Alice always loved talking about her cat Dinah and how good she was at catching mice and chasing after birds. She was rather surprised to find her speech was causing quite a commotion amongst the party. Some of the animals started hurrying off. Soon, Alice was left alone. "I wish I hadn't mentioned Dinah!" she said to herself sadly.

Alice was beginning to cry, when she heard a pattering of feet in the distance. She looked up, half hoping that the Mouse had changed his mind and was coming back to finish his story. But instead it was the White Rabbit looking anxiously as if he'd lost something and muttering to himself, "The Duchess! Oh, my dear paws! Oh, my fur and whiskers! She'll get me executed for sure! Where can I have dropped them, I wonder?"

Alice guessed in a moment that he must be looking for his fan and white gloves, and she began looking for them, but they were nowhere to be seen. Everything seemed to have changed since her swim in the pool, and the great hall with the glass table and the little door had vanished completely.

The Rabbit noticed Alice looking about and called out to her in an angry voice, "Why, Mary Ann, what are you doing out here? Run home at once and fetch me a pair of gloves and a fan! Quick, now!"

Alice was too frightened to explain that she was Alice, not Mary Ann (who she supposed must have been the Rabbit's servant) and ran off in the direction he was pointing in.

"How surprised he'll be when he finds out who I am!" Alice thought. "But I'd better take him his fan and gloves—if I can find them." Just then she came across a little house, with a brass plate on the door with the name "W. RABBIT" engraved on it. She went in without knocking, and hurried upstairs, afraid that she might meet the real Mary Ann and be turned away before she'd found the fan and gloves.

"How strange it seems," Alice said to herself, "to be doing errands for a rabbit!"

By this time, Alice had come to a tidy little room with a table by the window, and on it (as she'd hoped) a fan and two or three pairs of tiny white leather gloves. She picked up a pair of gloves with the fan and was just about to leave the room, when she spied a little bottle standing next to the mirror. There was no label this time saying "DRINK ME" but nevertheless, she uncorked it and had a little sip. "Something interesting seems to happen whenever I eat or drink anything lately, so I'll just see what this bottle does. I do hope it'll make me grow large again. I'm really quite tired of being so small!"

MAKE A WATER CYCLE

Discover how liquid water evaporates into water vapor and how this process can be sped up or slowed down.

1

Using the permanent marker, decorate the top half of your clear plastic bag with clouds to make it look like the sky.

YOU WILL NEED:

- Clear, plastic zip-lock bag
- Permanent marker
- Cup of water
- Blue food coloring
- Spoon
- Clear tape

2

Add a few drops of food coloring to the cup of water and mix with a spoon.

3

Carefully pour the cup of water into your bag and tightly seal the top.

4

Using tape, stick the bag onto the inside of a window. The sunnier the window, the better the results will be.

5

Can you see water droplets gathering at the top of the bag, in the clouds? How did they get there?

6

Leave the bag for a few hours, then check to see if anything has happened. What happens to the bag after a cold, dark night?

WHY IT WORKS

Depending on how warm your window is, some water will have evaporated inside the bag. As it evaporates, it turns from a liquid into a gas, and floats to the top of the bag. The warmer the window, the faster the water will evaporate. This mimics Earth's natural water cycle, where water evaporates from the planet's surface to form clouds, before eventually falling as rain.

MAKE A WORD PICTURE

Use your imagination to create a picture out of words. The words you choose can make as much or as little sense as you like. Try using a pet or family member as inspiration and choosing words that remind you of your subject.

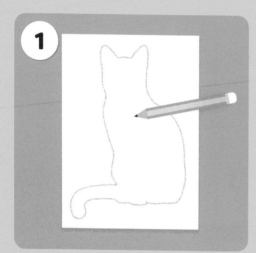

1

Choose a subject for your word picture. It could be anything that inspires you. Draw an outline of your picture on the piece of cardstock.

YOU WILL NEED:

- Pencil
- Piece of printer-size cardstock
- Old magazines and newspapers
- Scissors
- Glue
- Felt-tip pens (optional)

2

Search through the old magazines and newspapers for any words and phrases that jump out at you. Carefully cut these out and keep them safe.

TIP

Can you find lighter colors for the highlights in your picture? And darker images for the shadows?

3

Start laying your words and phrases on top of the cardstock, filling in the outline of your picture.

4

GLUE

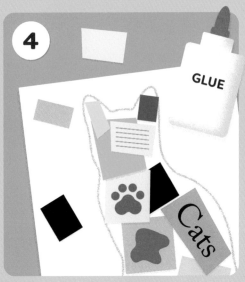

Once you're happy with your word picture, start gluing down the pieces of paper to create a collage of words.

5

Fill in any gaps with handwritten words using felt-tip pens, if you want to. Think about the colors that you use and how they relate to the picture.

TAKE IT FURTHER

Try creating a collage using more materials and different textures. Start by collecting materials that remind you of your chosen subject. Pictures from magazines, old wrapping paper, and natural materials, such as leaves and feathers, might work well. Then, repeat steps 3 to 5 as before.

Chapter 4

Bill to the Rescue

As if the drink was reading her mind, and much sooner than she expected, Alice found her head was pressed against the ceiling and she was having to stoop to fit in. She'd only drunk half the bottle and quickly put it down. "That's quite enough, I hope I don't grow any more! As it is, there's no way I can get out of the door! I wish I hadn't drunk quite so much."

But it was too late. Alice went on growing and growing and very soon she had to kneel down on the floor. After another minute, there wasn't enough room even for this, and she tried lying down with one elbow against the door and the other arm curled around her head. Still she went on growing. In desperation, Alice put one arm out of the window and one foot up the chimney and said to herself, "Now I can do no more, whatever happens. Oh, dear!"

Thankfully, the drink had now taken its full effect and Alice didn't grow any larger. She was still very uncomfortable though, and had no idea how she was ever going to get out of the room again.

"Life was much easier at home," thought Alice, "when I wasn't always growing larger and smaller, and being ordered about by mice and rabbits. I almost wish I'd not gone down that rabbit hole, and yet, this sort of life is rather curious! I wonder what on earth happened to me!

When I used to read fairy tales, I thought this kind of thing never really happened, and now here I am in the middle of one! There ought to be a book written about me for sure! And when I grow up, I'll write one ... but I seem to be grown up now," she added sadly, "at least, there's no room to grow up any more here!"

"But then," thought Alice, "shall I never get any older than I am now? There's some comfort in that—never to be an old woman, but then, always to have lessons to learn. Oh, I wouldn't like that!"

"Oh, don't be foolish, Alice!" she answered herself. "How can you learn lessons in here? There's hardly any room for you, let alone any textbooks." And so she went on, taking one side of the argument and then the other, and making quite a conversation of it. But after a few minutes, she heard a voice outside and stopped to listen.

"Mary Ann! Mary Ann!" said the voice. "Fetch my gloves this instant!" Then there was a little pattering of feet on the stairs.

 ## RETURNING THE RABBIT'S FAN

In all the commotion, Alice forgets that the White Rabbit is waiting for his fan and gloves. Will she ever be able to escape from the room?

Turn to page 56 to make a new fan for the White Rabbit, using colored paper and a few simple measurements.

Alice knew it was the Rabbit coming to look for her. As she trembled, the whole house shook. She'd quite forgotten that she was now about a thousand times larger than the Rabbit, and needn't be afraid.

The Rabbit came up to the door and tried to open it, but Alice's elbow was pressing so hard against it, he couldn't get in. Alice heard him say to himself, "Then I'll go around and get in through the window."

"You won't be able to do that!" thought Alice. After waiting for a while, she thought she heard the Rabbit just under the window. She heard a little shriek and a fall, a crash of breaking glass, and she imagined the Rabbit must have fallen into the greenhouse or something.

Then an angry voice—the Rabbit's—"Pat! Pat! Where are you?" And then a voice she'd never heard before, "Sure, I'm here! Digging for apples, sir!"

"Digging for apples, indeed!" said the Rabbit angrily. "Here! Come and help me out of this!" Then more sounds of breaking glass.

"Now tell me, Pat, what's that in the window?"

"I'm sure it's an arm, sir."

CONTROL AND COORDINATION

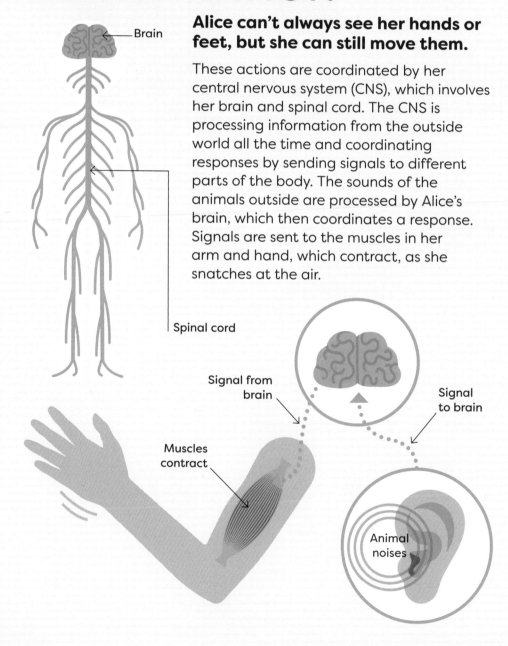

Brain

Alice can't always see her hands or feet, but she can still move them.

These actions are coordinated by her central nervous system (CNS), which involves her brain and spinal cord. The CNS is processing information from the outside world all the time and coordinating responses by sending signals to different parts of the body. The sounds of the animals outside are processed by Alice's brain, which then coordinates a response. Signals are sent to the muscles in her arm and hand, which contract, as she snatches at the air.

Spinal cord

Signal from brain

Signal to brain

Muscles contract

Animal noises

"An arm? Whoever saw one that size? Why it fills the whole window!"

"Sure, it does, sir, but it's definitely an arm."

"Well, it's got no business to be there. Go and take it away!"

There was a long silence after this. Alice could only hear whispers now and then. Alice spread out her hand and snatched at the air. There were two little shrieks, and more sounds of breaking glass. "Whatever is going on down there?" she thought. "As for pulling me out of the window, I wish they could! I really don't want to stay in here any longer."

Alice waited for some time without hearing any more. At last, there was a rumbling of little cartwheels, and lots of voices talking at once. Alice could make out a few words: "Where's the other ladder?"—"Bill's got the other. Bill! Fetch it here, lad!"—"They don't reach high enough yet"—"Oh! They'll do well enough."—"Here, Bill. Catch hold of the rope!"—"Mind that loose slate!"—"Oh, it's coming down, watch out!" followed by a loud crash. "Who will go down the chimney?"—"I shan't!"—"Bill will go down! Here, Bill! The master says you're to go down the chimney!"

"Oh, so Bill's got to go down the chimney, has he?" Alice said to herself. "They seem to put everything upon Bill! I wouldn't be in Bill's place for anything. This fireplace is very narrow, but perhaps I can kick a little."

Alice drew her foot as far down the chimney as she could and waited until she heard a little animal (she wasn't sure what animal Bill was) scratching and scrambling about in the chimney close above her. Then she gave a sharp kick and waited to see what happened next.

She heard a crowd shout, "There goes Bill!" then the Rabbit's voice saying, "Catch him, you by the hedge!" then silence. Finally, some confused voices, "Hold up his head"—"Give him some brandy"—"Don't choke him!"—"How was it, old fellow? Whatever happened?"

At last, a feeble squeaking voice replied ("That's Bill," Alice thought). "Well, I hardly know. Something came at me like a Jack-in-the-box, and then I went up like a rocket!"

"You sure did!" the others agreed.

"We must burn the house down!" said the Rabbit's voice, and Alice called out as loud as she could, "I'll set Dinah on you if you do!"

There was a stunned silence. "I wonder what they'll do next?" Alice thought. "If they had any sense, they'd take the roof off." After a minute or two they began moving about again and Alice heard the Rabbit say, "A barrowful will do to begin with."

"A barrowful of what?" Alice thought. But she didn't have to wait long. A shower of pebbles came flying through the window, with some hitting her face! "I'll put a stop to this," she said to herself, and shouted out, "You'd better not do that again!" Another stunned silence.

HOW FAR CAN A LIZARD FLY?

Air resistance ⟶

Bill's flight path ⟶

Acceleration ⟶

Gravity pulls down

← Air resistance

Bill's flight path depends on the strength of Alice's kick and the forces acting upon him as he flies through the air.

When Alice kicks at the chimney, the force of the kick determines the speed and direction of Bill's acceleration out of the chimney. Air resistance (drag) acts in the opposite direction to motion, slowing Bill down. Gravity acts on Bill's mass, pulling him toward the center of Earth, until he eventually hits the ground.

To her surprise, Alice noticed that the pebbles were turning into little cakes as they lay on the floor. She had a bright idea. "If I eat one of these cakes," she thought to herself, "maybe I'll shrink. It surely can't make me any larger."

Alice gulped down one of the cakes and was delighted to find she started shrinking immediately. As soon as she was small enough to get through the door, she dashed out of the house, and found quite a crowd of little animals and birds waiting outside. Bill (who she discovered was a little lizard) was in the middle, being held up by two guinea-pigs, who were giving him something from a bottle. They all rushed at Alice the moment she appeared, but she ran off as fast as she could, and soon found herself safe between the trees of a thick forest.

"The first thing I've got to do," Alice said to herself, "is to grow to my right size again. The second thing is to find my way into that lovely garden."

It sounded like a good idea, but the only problem was Alice didn't have a clue how to set about it. While she was peering among the

SHRINKING EGGS

Alice is desperate to shrink back to her normal size, but it's not an easy task. Shrinking an egg, on the other hand, is much simpler.

Turn to page 58 to grow and shrink some eggs by placing them in different liquids. If only Alice were as easy to change in size!

trees, she heard a little bark just above her head which made her look up in a hurry. An enormous puppy was looking down at her with large round eyes, stretching out one of its paws to touch her. "Poor little thing!" Alice said in a friendly tone. She tried hard to whistle to it but was also frightened the puppy might be hungry, in which case it could possibly eat her up, even though she was trying to be nice.

Without any thought, Alice picked up a small stick and held it out to the puppy, who leapt into the air with a yelp of delight and rushed at the stick. Alice dodged behind a great thistle to avoid being run over. As soon as she appeared on the other side, the puppy rushed again at the stick, tumbling head over heels in excitement. At every moment, Alice expected to be trampled under his feet, and ran around the thistle again. The puppy kept coming back for the stick and barking hoarsely each time, until at last, he sat down to rest a little way off, panting with his tongue hanging out of his mouth and his great eyes half shut.

This seemed like a good time for Alice to escape. She ran until she was out of breath and the puppy's bark sounded faint. "It was a dear little puppy though!" Alice thought, as she rested against a buttercup and fanned herself with one of the leaves. "I would have liked teaching it tricks, if only I'd been the right size to do so! Oh dear! I'd nearly forgotten that I've got to grow up again! How shall I do it? I suppose I ought to eat or drink something, but the question is—what?"

MAKE A PAPER FAN

Recreate the White Rabbit's fan with colorful paper and ice pop sticks. Decorate your fan with a Wonderland-inspired design of your choice.

1

Decorate your paper with the coloring pens, pencils, or paints.

YOU WILL NEED:

- Large piece of paper, about 3 ft (1 m) by 8 in (20 cm)
- Coloring pens, pencils, or paints
- 2 popsicle sticks
- White glue
- Tape

2

Take one of the shortest edges of the paper and fold it over, creating a fold that is about 0.6 in (1.5 cm) wide.

3

Turn the paper over and fold it back on itself, creating a pleat. Keep turning and folding the paper along its width until the entire length of paper is pleated.

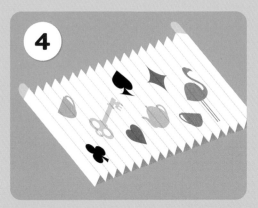

Glue a popsicle stick to each end of the paper, leaving a 0.8 in (2 cm) gap of paper on one side. This is the bottom of the fan. The sticks should stick out slightly over the top edge of the fan.

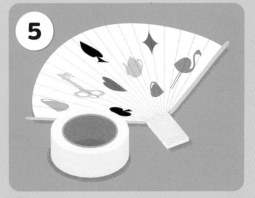

Pinch the paper at the bottom of the fan together and wrap a small amount of tape around the end to secure.

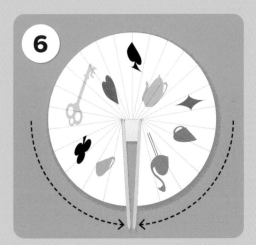

When the glue is dry, open up your fan by pulling the popsicle sticks all the way around until they meet.

WHY IT WORKS

The White Rabbit is always in a hurry. No wonder he needs a fan to keep cool! Using a fan creates a cooling effect, like a breeze. It replaces hot, humid air with cooler, drier air.

SHRINK AND GROW EGGS

As if by magic, you can make an egg shrink or swell in size! All you need is two eggs, some vinegar, molasses, and a little patience.

1

First, you need to remove the shells of the delicate eggs without breaking them. To do this, pour 7 oz (200 ml) of vinegar into each of the two beakers or tall glasses. Place one egg in each beaker of vinegar and leave to soak for 24 hours.

YOU WILL NEED:

- 14 oz (400 ml) vinegar
- 4 beakers or tall glasses
- 2 eggs
- Tongs (optional)
- 7 oz (200 ml) molasses
- 7 oz (200 ml) water

2

The next day, you should find two "naked eggs" sitting in the vinegar—their shells have dissolved! Carefully remove the eggs from the vinegar and gently wash away any remaining shell if needed.

TIP

Keep a cloth or some paper towels handy—this might get messy!

3

Fill another beaker with the water and the fourth beaker with the molasses.

4

Place one of the "naked eggs" in the water and the other in the molasses. Leave them to soak again overnight.

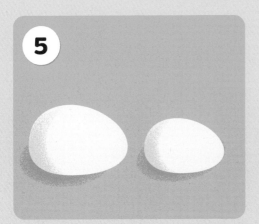

5

What do you notice about the appearance of the eggs? Is one egg noticeably smaller than the other?

WHY IT WORKS

The egg soaked in molasses will have shrunk, whereas the egg in water may have swollen up. Water molecules move from a high concentration of water to a low concentration of water due to a process called "osmosis." Molasses has a low concentration of water, so the water molecules in the egg move across the egg's membrane and into the molasses, making the egg shrink. Why might the egg sitting in the water have grown?

Chapter 5

Advice from a Caterpillar

Alice looked around at the flowers and blades of grass. She couldn't see anything that looked like the right thing to eat or drink under the circumstances. There was a large mushroom growing near, at her height, and when she looked under it, and on both sides of it, and behind it, she thought she might as well look on top, too!

Alice stretched herself up on tiptoe and peeped over the edge of the mushroom. Her eyes met those of a large caterpillar sitting on top, not taking the slightest notice of her or anything else around him. The Caterpillar and Alice looked at each other for some time without saying a word. At last, the Caterpillar said in a sleepy voice, "Who are *you*?"

This was a difficult conversation starter. Alice wasn't entirely sure at that moment who she was! "I'm not sure, sir, just at the moment. At least I know who I was when I got up this morning, but I think I've been changed several times since then."

"Whatever do you mean?" the Caterpillar replied sternly. "Explain yourself, please!"

"I can't I'm afraid, sir, because I'm not myself, you see."

"I don't see," said the Caterpillar.

"I'm afraid I can't put it more clearly," Alice replied politely, "for I can't understand it myself to begin with! And being so many different sizes in a day is very confusing."

"It isn't," said the Caterpillar.

"Well perhaps you don't think so at the moment," said Alice, "but when you turn into a chrysalis one day, and after that into a butterfly, I expect you'll find it rather strange."

"Not a bit," said the Caterpillar.

"Well, perhaps you feel differently than me," said Alice. "All I know is, I would find it very strange!"

"You!" said the Caterpillar disdainfully. "Anyway, who are *you*?"

GEOMETRIC ART

Have you noticed how nature features some extraordinary patterns?

Think of the colorful markings on a caterpillar, the symmetry of a butterfly's wings, or the repeating pattern that makes up the center of a flower.

Turn to page 70 to create your own beautiful repeating patterns using a compass, colorful pencils, and simple math!

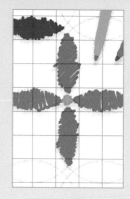

PATTERNS IN NATURE

What do you notice about this sequence?

0, 1, 1, 2, 3, 5, 8, 13, 21, 34, 55, 89, 144 ...

Each number is the sum of the two previous ones.
So, 0 + 1 = 1, 1 + 1 = 2, 1 + 2 = 3, 2 + 3 = 5, etc.
This is named the Fibonacci Sequence. It is named
after a mathematician called Fibonacci, who noticed
that this sequence has a special place in nature.

If we draw this pattern, it looks like this:

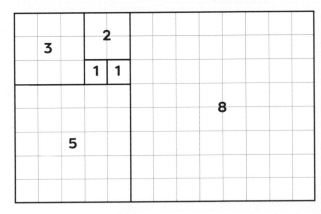

Then, if you draw
a curved line from
the smallest square,
curving from corner
to corner through
each box away from
the center, we get a
spiral. This is called
the "golden spiral" and
it's seen everywhere—
from the shape of a
seashell to the way
a caterpillar curls its
body and the spiraling
center of a daisy.

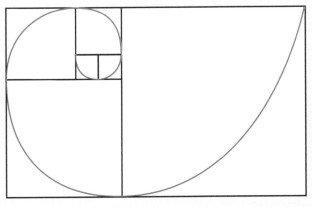

Seashell

This took them back to their first conversation. Alice was beginning to feel a little irritated and she said sternly, "I think you ought to tell me who *you* are, first."

"Why?" said the Caterpillar.

Alice couldn't actually think of a good reason why, and as the Caterpillar seemed to be in an unpleasant mood, she turned away.

"Come back!" the Caterpillar called after her. "I've got something important to say!"

This sounded promising, so Alice turned back again.

"Keep your temper," the Caterpillar said.

"Is that all?" Alice said, trying not to let her anger bubble over.

"No," said the Caterpillar. Alice thought she might as well wait as she had nothing else to do. Perhaps the Caterpillar would tell her something worth hearing. After a while, the Caterpillar sighed and said, "So you think you're changed, do you?"

"I'm afraid I am, sir," Alice replied. "I can't remember things anymore, and I can't keep my size for more than ten minutes!"

"Can't remember what things?" said the Caterpillar.

"Well, I've tried to recite various verses, but they always come out wrong!" Alice replied sadly.

"Try the poem *You are old, Father William*," the Caterpillar suggested.

Alice folded her hands and began to recite the words.

"That wasn't right at all," the Caterpillar remarked.

"No, you see," Alice replied. "I just can't seem to get the words right."

"What size do you want to be?" the Caterpillar asked.

"I don't really mind, to be honest," Alice replied, "as long as I don't keep changing, you know."

"I don't know," said the Caterpillar. Alice was beginning to lose her temper.

"Are you happy now?" the Caterpillar said.

"Well, it would be nice to be a little larger, sir, if you wouldn't mind," said Alice. "Three inches is rather an annoying height to be."

"It's a very good height!" said the Caterpillar angrily, pulling himself upright as he spoke (he was exactly three inches high).

"But I'm not used it!" Alice explained, wishing that all these creatures weren't so easily offended.

"You'll get used to it in time," said the Caterpillar, lying down again.

MEMORY GAMES

How could Alice improve her memory?

Alice will only be able to recall poems at a later date if they are stored in her long-term memory.

• The brain is taking in information all the time through the five main senses (the sensory memory) and only some of this information is transferred to the short-term memory.

• The short-term memory can only hold about seven items for 30 seconds.

• There are methods to help turn a short-term memory into a long-term memory, including rehearsing information, organizing information, and adding extra details such as sights, smells, and sounds.

Perhaps Alice could use one of these techniques to remember her poems in the future.

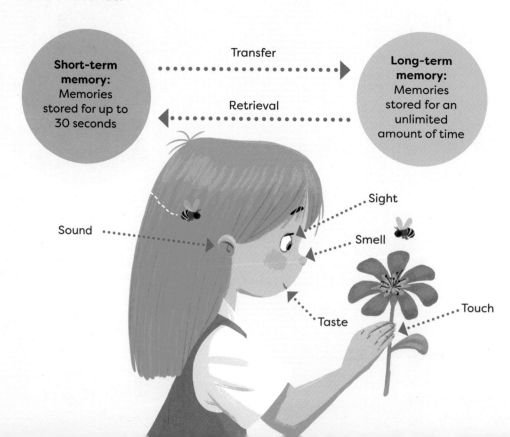

Short-term memory:
Memories stored for up to 30 seconds

Transfer

Retrieval

Long-term memory:
Memories stored for an unlimited amount of time

Sound

Sight

Smell

Taste

Touch

Alice waited patiently this time, and after a minute or two the Caterpillar began to crawl down off the mushroom and slither into the grass. As he went, he remarked, "One side will make you grow taller, the other side will make you grow shorter."

"One side of what? The other side of what?" Alice thought to herself.

"Of the mushroom," said the Caterpillar, as if she'd said her thought aloud, and with that he was out of sight.

Alice looked at the mushroom for a while, trying to work out the two sides, as the mushroom was perfectly round. Eventually, she stretched her arms around it as far as they would go and broke off a bit with each hand. "The only trouble now is, which is which?" she said to herself. She nibbled some of the right-hand bit. Before she knew it, she felt a violent blow beneath her chin—it had struck her foot!

Alice was shocked at this sudden change but felt there was no time to lose because she was shrinking rapidly. She began to eat some of the other bit. Her chin was pressed so closely against her foot, there was hardly any room to open her mouth! But she finally managed to swallow a little of the left-hand bit.

"Thank goodness, my head is free!" said Alice. But before she knew it, her shoulders were nowhere to be found. All she could see was a long neck which seemed to rise like a stalk out of a sea of green leaves.

"Wherever have my shoulders gone? And my poor hands, I can't see them at all!" Alice was moving her hands as she spoke, which caused a little shaking among the distant tree leaves.

Alice was delighted to find that her neck bent easily in any direction, like a snake! She had just managed to curve her neck down and was going to dive among the trees, when a large pigeon flew into her face, beating her violently with its wings.

"Snake, I say!" screamed the Pigeon, adding sadly, "I've tried everything but nothing seems to suit them! I've tried the roots of trees, and I've tried banks and hedges," the Pigeon went on, "but those snakes! There's no pleasing them! As if it wasn't trouble enough hatching my eggs, I must be on the lookout for snakes day and night! Why, I haven't had a wink of sleep these last three weeks!"

"I'm very sorry to hear that," said Alice.

"And just as I was thinking I should be free of them at last," continued the Pigeon, "they come wriggling down from the sky! Ugh, snakes!"

"But I'm not a snake, I promise you!" said Alice. "I'm a… I'm a…

 FLOATING ARMS

Try this: raise your arm. Now drop it back down. Easy, right?

Not for Alice—she finds it difficult to move body parts like her neck. Usually, your brain tells the parts of your body when to move, but this isn't always the case.

Turn to page 72 to find out how to trick your arms into moving without you telling them to.

I'm a little girl," said Alice, rather doubtfully, as she remembered the number of changes she'd gone through that day.

"A likely story indeed!" said the Pigeon. "I've seen a good many little girls, but never one with such a neck as that! No! You're a snake. I suppose you'll be telling me next that you've never tasted an egg!"

"I have tasted eggs," said Alice, who was a very truthful child, "but little girls eat eggs as much as snakes do, you see."

"I don't believe it," said the Pigeon, "but if they do, they must be a kind of snake, that's all I can say."

"Well, be off, then!" said the Pigeon sulkily, as she settled down again in her nest. Alice crouched down among the trees, but her neck kept getting tangled in the branches and every now and then, she had to untwist it. After a while, she remembered that she still held the pieces of mushroom in her hands, and she set to work very carefully, nibbling first at one and then at the other, and growing sometimes taller and sometimes shorter, until she had succeeded in bringing herself down to her normal size.

It was so long since Alice had been anything like her right size, that it felt quite strange at first. But she soon got used to it and began cheering herself along. "Come on, that's half the plan done already! How puzzling all these changes are. But I've gotten back to my right size, and the next thing is to get into the beautiful garden. But how is that to be done?"

GEOMETRIC ART

Create repeating patterns using graph paper and simple calculations. Do these patterns look like anything you would see in nature?

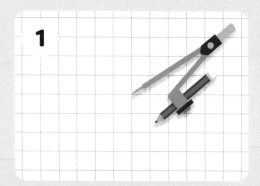

1

Secure your pencil into the compass and place the point of the compass at the center of the graph paper, in a position where two grid lines cross over.

YOU WILL NEED:

- Compass
- Pencil
- Graph paper
- Felt-tip pens

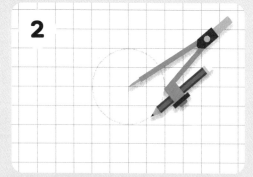

2

Draw a circle around the compass point with a radius (the distance between the compass point and the pencil lead) of two squares. Your circle should measure four boxes high and four boxes wide.

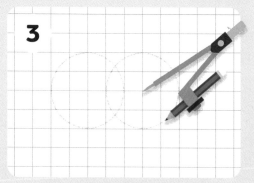

3

Move the compass point three boxes to the right and place the point down where the grid lines cross. Draw another circle with the same radius here. The second circle should overlap the first circle by one square.

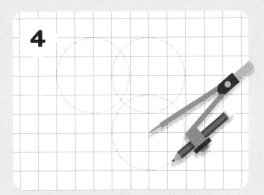

4

Count three boxes down and place the compass point on the paper. Draw another circle here. Can you see a repeating pattern forming?

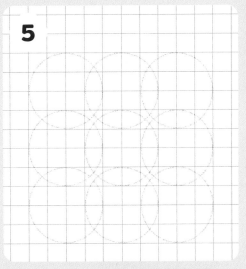

5

Keep repeating the process of moving three boxes to the left, right, up, and down until you have filled your paper with circles.

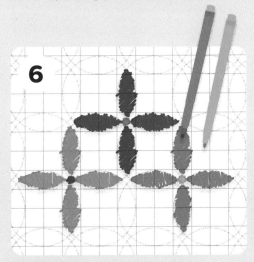

6

Use the felt-tip pens to color in your pattern. You could pick out the overlapping sections of the circles to look like the petals of flowers. Do you see any other patterns emerging?

WHY IT WORKS

By using the principles of geometry, you have created a simple repeating pattern. This kind of pattern, made up of identical shapes that are repeated over and over, can be seen all around us in nature. Take a look for geometric patterns in snowflakes, seashells, and flowers.

FLOATING ARMS

Can your arm move without a command from your brain? This experiment explores involuntary muscle contractions —when your muscles work outside of your control.

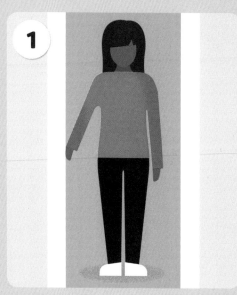

1

Stand in the open doorway with one arm pressed against the doorframe.

YOU WILL NEED:

- Open doorway
- Yourself
- Stopwatch, or timer on a phone (optional)

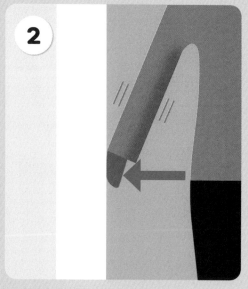

2

Press as hard as you can with the back of your hand into the doorframe, as if you're trying to push it away.

TIP

A stopwatch or timer on a phone can help you time yourself more accurately and compare your results.

3

60 SECONDS

Continue pushing hard as you count slowly for 60 seconds. Alternatively, you can use a stopwatch.

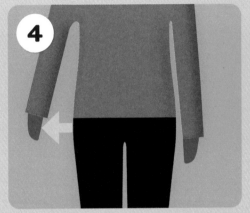

4

When the time is up, step away from the doorway and completely relax your arms down by your sides. Do you feel anything happening?

5

120 SECONDS

What happens if you push for longer than 60 seconds? Try out different lengths of time and see how this affects your results.

WHY IT WORKS

Usually, your brain commands your muscles to contract to create movement. In this experiment, a repeated action (pressing against the wall) for an extended period of time, triggers an involuntary muscle contraction that makes your arm lift up by itself!

Chapter 6

Pig and Pepper

Alice came across a little glade in the forest, with a house four feet high. "I wonder who lives there? I can't introduce myself at this size, I'd frighten the life out of them!" Alice thought. She began nibbling the right-hand side of the mushroom until she was nine inches high.

Alice was wondering what to do next, when a smartly dressed footman came running out of the forest—he was actually a fish. When he knocked at the door, another footman appeared—with a round face and large eyes like a frog. Alice crept a little farther away and listened.

The Fish-Footman produced a long letter from under his arm. He handed it to the other saying solemnly, "For the Duchess. An invitation from the Queen to play croquet." The footmen both had powdered hair curled all over their heads. When they both bowed low, it caused the curls to tangle together! This made Alice laugh so much, she had to run farther back in case they heard her laughter. When she next peeped out, the Fish-Footman had gone, and the other was sitting on the ground by the door, staring stupidly at the sky.

Alice approached the door cautiously and knocked.

"There's no use knocking," said the Footman, "and that's for two reasons. Firstly, I'm on the same side of the door as you, and secondly, they're making so much noise inside, no one will hear you."

It was true, there was a constant crying and sneezing, and every now and then a great crash, as if a dish or plate had been smashed to pieces.

"Please," said Alice, "how should I get in?"

The Footman replied, "There might be some sense in your knocking if the door was between us. If you were inside and I let you out, for example." He continued looking at the sky, which Alice thought rude.

"I shall sit here," the Footman remarked, "until tomorrow—" The door opened and a large plate skimmed past the Footman's head. "—or the next day, maybe," the Footman continued as if nothing had happened.

"How should I get in?" asked Alice again, even louder.

Alice found the Footman infuriating. "There's no use asking him, I'll just have to go in!"

Inside, the Duchess was sitting on a three-legged stool in the middle of a large kitchen, nursing a baby. A cook was leaning over the fire, stirring a large cauldron of soup.

"There's certainly too much pepper in that soup!" Alice said to herself, as she began to sneeze. Even the Duchess sneezed now and then, and as for the baby, it was sneezing and crying repeatedly. The only ones unaffected were the cook and a large, grinning cat.

SNEEZING ATTACK!

Sneezing is a clever way for your body to clear the nose of anything that shouldn't be there.

Whether it's dust, germs, pollution—or even pepper— the little hairs inside the nostrils get irritated and a signal is sent to the brain indicating that it's time to sneeze.

With a sneeze on the way, your body braces in preparation, then water, mucus, and air are forced out of the nose at speeds of up to 100 mph (161 kph)!

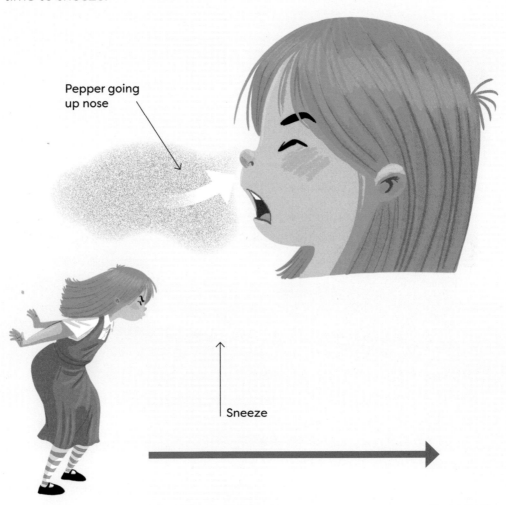

Pepper going up nose

Sneeze

"Please would you tell me," asked Alice timidly—she wasn't sure if it was polite for her to speak first, "why your cat grins like that?"

"It's a Cheshire cat," said the Duchess, "and that's why. Pig!"

The last word came out so strongly, it made Alice jump, but she realized it was meant for the baby, so she continued—

"I didn't know Cheshire cats always grinned. In fact, I didn't know that cats *could* grin."

"They all can," said the Duchess, "and most of them do."

"I don't know any that do," Alice said politely.

"You don't know much," said the Duchess, "and that's a fact."

Alice didn't like the way she said this and tried to change the subject. Meanwhile, the cook took the cauldron from the fire and began throwing everything within her reach at the Duchess and the baby— the fire tongs, saucepans, and some plates and dishes. The Duchess took no notice, even when they hit her, and the baby was crying so much already, it was difficult to know whether the blows hurt or not.

"Oh, please stop!" cried Alice. She glanced at the cook, who seemed not to be listening. The Duchess began nursing the child again, singing a kind of lullaby (although it wasn't very soothing):

"Speak roughly to your little boy and beat him when he sneezes.
He only does it to annoy, because he knows it teases."

While the Duchess sang the second verse, the baby kept crying and Alice could hardly hear the words.

"Here! You may nurse him for a bit, if you like!" the Duchess passed the baby to Alice. "I must get ready to play croquet with the Queen." As she hurried off, the cook threw a frying-pan after her, but luckily it just missed.

Alice took the baby, who was a strange little creature—his arms and legs sticking out in all directions. "Just like a starfish," she thought. The poor little thing was snorting like a steam engine and wriggling so much it was all Alice could do to keep hold of him.

When the baby settled a little, she took him outside for some fresh air. "If I don't take this child away," thought Alice, "he'll surely come to harm. It must be the right thing to do." The little thing grunted as if in reply.

When he grunted again, Alice looked anxiously at his face to see what the matter was. There could be no doubt the baby had a *very* turned-up nose, more like a snout than a real nose. His eyes were also getting extremely small for a baby. Alice didn't like the sight of him at all. "Perhaps he's just sobbing," she thought, but there were no tears. "If you're going to turn into a pig, my dear," said Alice seriously, "I'll have nothing more to do with you!" The poor little thing sobbed again (or grunted, it was impossible to say which), and they went on for some time in silence.

Alice was thinking, "What on earth shall I do with this creature?" when he grunted again, so violently, that she looked down at his face with alarm. This time there could be *no* mistake—he was a pig!

Alice set the creature down and felt quite relieved to see him trot away into the forest, when the Cheshire Cat startled her, sitting on the bough of a tree a few yards away. The Cat grinned when he saw Alice. He looked friendly but did have *very* long claws and a great many teeth, so she thought it best to treat him with respect.

"Cheshire Puss," she began timidly. She wasn't sure if he would like that name, but he just grinned a little wider. "Would you tell me, please, which way I should go from here?"

"That depends on where you want to go," said the Cat.

"I don't really mind where," said Alice, "as long as I get *somewhere*."

"Oh, you'll do that," said the Cat, "if you only walk long enough."

 ## TRANSFORM A SHAPE

In Wonderland, babies can transform into pigs. In our world, we have to make do with the transformation of shapes.

Turn to page 84 to find out how to transform a shape through reflection.

Alice tried asking in another way.
"What sort of people live around here?"

"Over *there*," said the Cat, waving his right paw, "lives a Hatter, and over *there*," waving his left paw, "lives a March Hare. Visit either, they're both mad. We're all mad here. I'm mad. You're mad."

"How do you know I'm mad?" said Alice.

"You must be," said the Cat, "or you wouldn't be here."

"And how do you know you're mad?" Alice asked.

"To begin with," said the Cat, "a dog's not mad. Do you agree?"

"I suppose so," Alice said.

"Well," the Cat went on, "a dog growls when it's angry, and wags its tail when it's pleased. Now *I* growl when I'm pleased and wag my tail when I'm angry. Therefore, I'm mad."

"*I* call it purring, not growling," said Alice.

"Are you playing croquet with the Queen?" asked the Cat.

"I should like that very much," Alice replied, "but I haven't been invited."

"You'll see me there," said the Cat, and vanished.

THE MADNESS OF PURRING

Why do cats purr?

If you think that a cat only purrs when it's happy, think again! Cats purr for other reasons too...

• A cat may purr because it is hungry or injured. It's thought that by purring, a cat is able to soothe and even help heal itself.

• The sound is made by constricting the flow of air in the cat's throat, which creates a low vibration or "purr."

• Even some big cats, such as cheetahs, pumas, and wild cats, make purring sounds too!

Vibrating vocal chords

While Alice looked where the Cat had been, it suddenly reappeared.

"By the way, what happened to the baby?" said the Cat.

"It turned into a pig," Alice said quietly.

"I thought it would," said the Cat, and vanished again.

Alice walked on in the direction of the March Hare's house.
She looked up and there was the Cheshire Cat, sitting in a tree.

"Did you say pig, or fig?" said the Cat.

"I said pig," replied Alice, "and I wish you wouldn't keep appearing
and disappearing so suddenly, you make me feel quite giddy."

"All right," said the Cat, and this time he vanished quite slowly,
beginning with the end of his tail, and ending with his grin.

"Well! I've often seen a cat without a grin," thought Alice, "but a grin
without a cat! It's the most curious thing I've ever seen!"

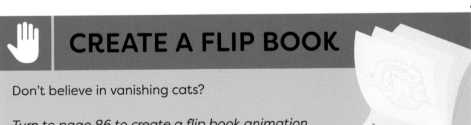

✋ CREATE A FLIP BOOK

Don't believe in vanishing cats?

*Turn to page 86 to create a flip book animation
and make the Cheshire Cat appear and
disappear at will.*

TRANSFORM A SHAPE

Shapes can be transformed in ways such as translation, rotation, reflection, and enlargement. Here's how to reflect a 2D shape.

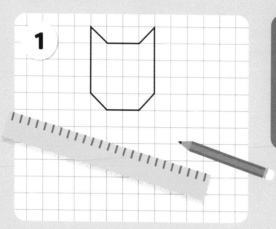

1

On your graph paper, plot a simple shape. Plot its corners where the lines of the graph paper cross.

YOU WILL NEED:

• Graph paper

• Pencil

• Ruler

• Tracing paper

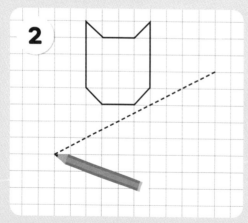

2

On one side of your shape, draw a long line across your paper using the ruler. This is called your "mirror line."

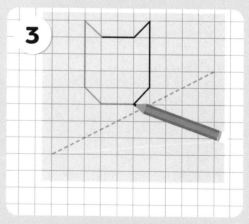

3

Place the tracing paper over your drawing and trace the original shape and mirror line through the paper.

TIP

You can use this method to draw reflections of more complex shapes, such as dodecagons (12-sided shapes), or even icosagons (20-sided shapes)!

4

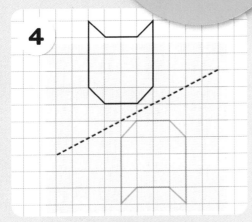

Flip your tracing paper over and position it on top of your original drawing so the mirror lines on both pieces of paper align (they should look like one single line).

5

Using the copied shape on your tracing paper as a guide, plot the corners (or vertices) of the reflected shape on the graph paper beneath.

6

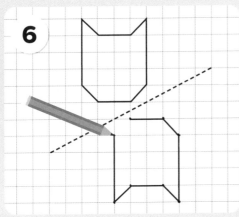

Join the dots together to create your reflected shape, using the ruler.

WHY IT WORKS

When you see yourself reflected in a mirror, both you and your reflection will appear to be an equal distance away from the mirror surface. In the same way, the corners, or vertices, of your reflected shape will be the same distance away from the mirror line as the vertices of your original shape.

PROJECT

CREATE A FLIP BOOK

Make a flip book animation of the Cheshire Cat appearing out of thin air, starting with his toothy grin...

1

On a scrap piece of paper, start by sketching a simple outline of the Cheshire Cat so you can see how the final image will look. You can trace the outline on this page as a reference if preferred.

YOU WILL NEED:

- Scrap piece of paper
- Sticky notes or small pad of paper
- Pencil
- Tracing paper (optional)

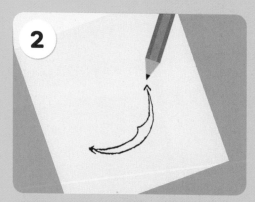

2

Turn to the back page of your sticky note pad. Start by drawing the outline of the Cheshire Cat's wide grin near the center of the paper.

3

Turn the page so that his grin is covered by one sheet of paper. Can you see the outline of the cat's grin through the paper? Trace this outline and add one extra detail, for example his sharp teeth.

TIP

To make a more detailed flip book animation, try adding details very gradually. By adding more pages to your flip book, the animation will be more detailed.

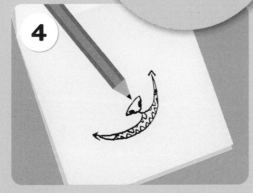

4

Turn the page again so that the second image is covered by one sheet of paper. Trace the outline of the second image and then add one extra detail, for example, the shape of the cat's nose.

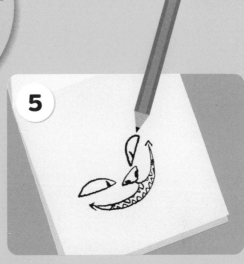

5

Keep turning the pages, working toward the front of the sticky note pad, adding one extra detail to the drawing each time, until you have completed the cat.

6

Place your flip book on a table and use your thumb to gradually flick through the pages, from the back to the front. Does your Cheshire Cat come to life?

WHY IT WORKS

By flicking quickly through the flip book, you are seeing a lot of pictures very fast. Your brain tries to make sense of this by "smoothing out" the images, filling in the gaps to create what looks like a continuous changing scene.

Chapter 7

A Mad Tea Party

It wasn't long before Alice found the March Hare's house. She thought it must be the right house, because the chimneys were shaped like ears and the roof was thatched with fur. She nibbled some of the left-hand piece of mushroom to raise herself to about two feet high.

A table was set out under a tree in the front garden where the March Hare and the Hatter were having tea. They were resting their elbows on a sleeping Dormouse sat between them. It was a large table, but the three of them were crowded together at one corner. "No room! No room!" they cried when they saw Alice coming. "There's *plenty* of room!" said Alice indignantly, and she sat down in a large armchair at one end of the table.

"It was rude of you to sit down without being invited," announced the March Hare.

"I didn't know it was *your* table," said Alice, "it's laid for a great many more than three."

"Your hair needs cutting," said the Hatter, after looking at Alice for some time.

"Don't make personal remarks," Alice scolded, "it's rude."

The Hatter opened his eyes very wide as she spoke, but all he said was, "Why is a raven like a writing-desk?"

"I believe I can guess that," replied Alice.

"Do you mean you think you know the answer? You should say what you mean," said the March Hare.

"I do," Alice replied, "at least, I mean what I say—that's the same thing, you know."

"Not the same thing at all!" said the Hatter. "You might as well say 'I see what I eat' is the same as 'I eat what I see'!"

"You might as well say," added the Dormouse, who seemed to be talking in his sleep, "'I breathe when I sleep' is the same as 'I sleep when I breathe'!"

"It *is* the same thing with you," the Hatter said to the Dormouse, and then the conversation stopped.

The Hatter was the first to break the silence. "What day of the month is it?" he asked, turning to Alice. He'd taken his watch from his pocket, and was shaking it now and then, and holding it to his ear.

"The fourth," Alice replied.

"Two days wrong!" sighed the Hatter. "I told you butter wouldn't suit the mechanism!" he added looking angrily at the March Hare.

"It was the *best* butter," the March Hare replied softly.

"Yes, but some crumbs must have got in as well," the Hatter grumbled.

The March Hare looked at the watch gloomily, dipped it into his tea, and looked at it again. "What a funny watch!" Alice said. "It tells the day of the month but not what o'clock it is!"

"Why should it?" muttered the Hatter. "Does *your* watch tell you the year?"

"Of course not," Alice replied, "but that's because it stays the same year for such a long time."

"Which is just the same with *mine*," said the Hatter.

"I don't quite understand," Alice said, as politely as she could.

"Have you guessed the riddle yet?" the Hatter said.

"No, I give up," Alice replied, "what's the answer?"

"I haven't the slightest idea," said the Hatter.

Alice sighed wearily. "Couldn't you do something better with the time," she said, "than waste it asking riddles that have no answers?"

TELLING THE TIME

The oldest time-telling devices are too big for us to carry around.

Thousands of years ago, people tracked the movements of the Sun, Moon, and stars in order to measure the passing of time. They created simple sundials, which were later developed into huge structures by the Ancient Romans. It wasn't until 700 years ago that mechanical clocks were invented. As the world became busier, inventors got to work creating more accurate clocks using a modern discovery: electricity. The most accurate clock today is the atomic clock, which should stay accurate within a second for 15 billion years!

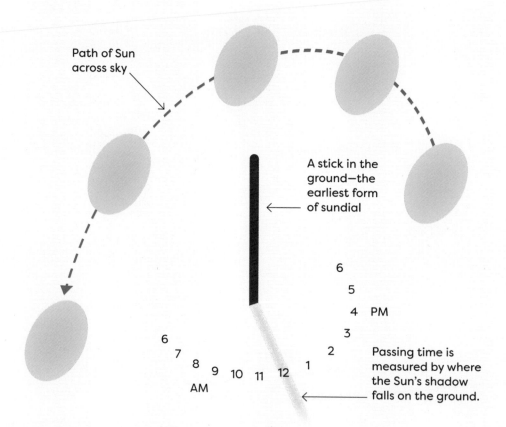

Path of Sun across sky

A stick in the ground—the earliest form of sundial

Passing time is measured by where the Sun's shadow falls on the ground.

6 5 4 PM 3 2 1 12 11 10 9 8 7 6 AM

"If you knew Time as well as I do," said the Hatter, "you wouldn't talk about wasting *it*. I don't suppose you've ever spoken to Time!"

"Perhaps not," Alice replied cautiously, "but I do beat time in music."

"Ah! He won't stand beating," said the Hatter. "We had a quarrel last March. It was at the great concert given by the Queen of Hearts, and I had to sing *'Twinkle, twinkle, little bat! How I wonder what you're at!'* Do you know that song?"

"I've heard something like it."

"Well, I'd hardly finished the first verse," said the Hatter, "when the Queen jumped up and bawled out. 'He's murdering the time! Off with his head!'"

"How awful!" exclaimed Alice.

"And ever since then," the Hatter went on sorrowfully, "he won't do a thing I ask! It's always six o'clock now."

MAKE A SUNDIAL

Losing time, killing time, wasting time ... We use time in all sorts of ways, but where does the measurement of time originate?

Turn to page 98 to make a sundial— humankind's earliest time-telling device.

An idea came into Alice's head. "Is that why so many tea-things are laid out here?" she asked.

"That's right," said the Hatter with a sigh, "it's always tea-time, and we've no time to wash the dishes."

"Then you keep moving around places, I suppose?" said Alice.

"Exactly," said the Hatter.

"Could we change the subject," the March Hare interrupted, yawning. "I'm getting tired of this. I vote the young lady tells us a story."

"I'm afraid I don't know one," said Alice, rather alarmed.

"Then the Dormouse shall!" they both cried. "Wake up, Dormouse!"

The Dormouse slowly opened his eyes. "I wasn't asleep," he said in a weak, hoarse voice. "I heard everything you said."

"Tell us a story!" said the March Hare. "And be quick about it," added the Hatter, "or you'll fall asleep again before it's done."

"Once upon a time, there were three little sisters," the Dormouse began in a great hurry, "and their names were Elsie, Lacie, and Tillie, and they lived at the bottom of a well—"

"What did they live on?" asked Alice, who was always interested in food and drink.

The Dormouse thought for a minute or two. "They lived on molasses," he said.

"They'd have been ill!" said Alice.

"So they were," said the Dormouse.

"But why did they live at the bottom of a well?" Alice enquired.

"Take some more tea," the March Hare said to Alice, earnestly.

"I haven't had any yet," Alice replied, rather offended, "so I can't take more."

"You mean you can't take *less*," said the Hatter, "it's very easy to take *more* than nothing."

Alice didn't know quite what to say to this, so she helped herself to some tea and bread-and-butter, and turned back to the Dormouse, "Why did they live at the bottom of a well?"

The Dormouse thought for a minute, "It was a molasses-well."

"There's no such thing!" Alice was feeling frustrated now, but the Hatter and March Hare went "Sh! Sh!" and the Dormouse remarked sulkily, "If you can't be nice, you'd better finish the story yourself."

"No, please go on!" said Alice humbly, "I won't interrupt again."

"I want a clean cup," interrupted the Hatter, "let's all move one place."

He moved on and the others followed. The Hatter was the only one to benefit from the change—and Alice was much worse off than before, because the March Hare had just spilled some milk on his plate.

Before long, the Dormouse fell asleep again. The others didn't seem to notice as Alice slipped away from the table.

"I shall never go *there* again!" said Alice, looking back in disgust.

As she walked away through the forest, she noticed one of the trees had a little door. "How curious," she thought. "But everything's curious today. I may as well go in!" and so she did.

Alice found herself back in the long hall once more, by the little glass table. "I should be able to manage better this time," she said to herself, as she took the little golden key and began unlocking the door that led into the garden.

TAKING TURNS

As the Hatter, March Hare, Dormouse and Alice change places, they are rotating around the table.

Turn to page 100 to create intricate patterns by rotating simple shapes.

USING PERSPECTIVE IN DRAWINGS

All art made before the 15th century has one thing in common—it lacks a sense of perspective.

This makes everything look rather flat, whereas in more recent art (and in photography), the lines within an image tend to lead toward a single point in the background. This is called the vanishing point. As objects get closer to the vanishing point, they look smaller, until they vanish completely.

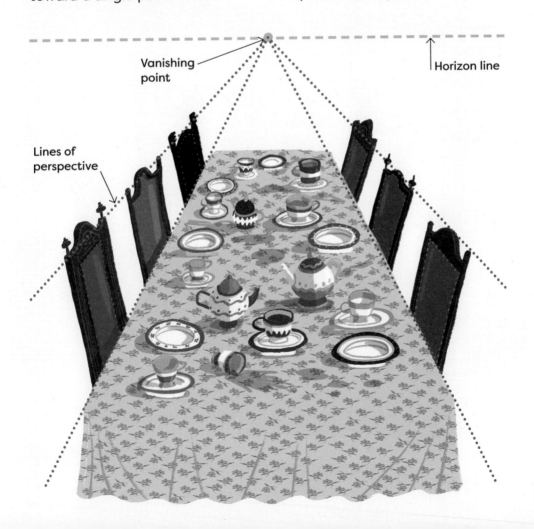

Vanishing point

Horizon line

Lines of perspective

MAKE A SUNDIAL

Measure time just as people did thousands of years ago. All it takes is a stick, a sunny day, and some patience!

1

YOU WILL NEED:
- Plant pot filled with soil
- Tall stick
- Chalk
- Clock or watch
- Sunny place

Place your pot of soil in a bright, sunny place outdoors. You'll need enough space around the pot to draw a ring of numbers.

2

Push the stick into the soil so that it points straight upward. Make sure it's secure and isn't going to topple over.

3

Keep an eye on the clock. When it reaches an hour mark, such as 12 o'clock, be ready to act! Can you see the stick's shadow moving as the Sun moves?

TIP

If you're working on grass, use a large sheet of paper and pens instead of chalk. Make sure you weigh the paper down so it doesn't blow away!

4

At each hour, use the chalk to mark the point where the shadow falls on the ground.

5

Write the hour next to the mark you just made, for example, if it's 12 o'clock, write "12."

6

At each hour, repeat this process of marking where the shadow falls until your sundial is as complete as possible.

WHY IT WORKS

You can use your sundial tomorrow to tell the time using the numbers marked on the ground. As the Sun moves across the sky, the shadow cast by the stick aligns with the different hour marks—which tells you roughly what time it is.

TAKING TURNS

Rotation patterns may look complex, but they're surprisingly simple to create. Color your pattern to make it even more spectacular.

1

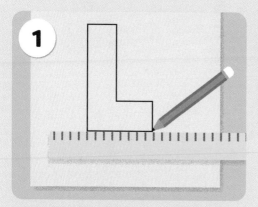

YOU WILL NEED:
- Ruler • Cardstock
- Pencil • Scissors
- Paper • Drawing pin

Use the ruler to draw an "L" shape on your cardstock, as shown. The longest side should measure roughly 4 in (10 cm).

2

With the help of an adult, carefully cut out your shape.

3

Place the cardstock shape on a piece of paper and poke the pin through both the cardstock and the paper (make sure the surface underneath is protected!).

TIP

Try moving the pin to a different part of your shape to create a new pattern, or, cut out a new shape entirely.

4

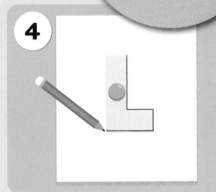

Hold the shape still with one hand. With the other, use the pencil to draw around the outline of the shape onto the paper below.

5

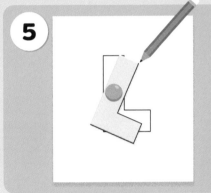

Keep the drawing pin where it is and rotate the shape by a little bit. You can now draw another "L" shape that is overlapping the first.

6

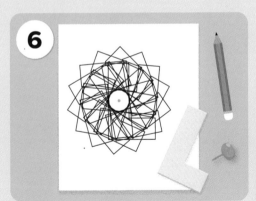

Keep rotating the cardstock shape, drawing around it each time, until you have a complete ring of overlapping shapes. Once you're happy with your pattern, take out the pin and color it in!

WHY IT WORKS

This type of pattern is created by rotating a shape around a fixed point. The shape stays exactly the same for each pattern, but its position in space will change. In math, this is called "rotation."

Chapter 8

The Queen's Croquet Ground

Alice began to nibble the piece of mushroom she'd kept in her pocket until she was about a foot high. She walked down the little passage and found herself—at last—in the beautiful garden, among the bright flowerbeds and the cool fountains.

A large rose tree stood near the garden's entrance. The roses were white, but three gardeners were busily painting them red. As Alice approached, she heard one of them say, "Look out now, Five! Don't go splashing paint over me like that!"

"I couldn't help it," said Five, sulkily. "Seven jogged my elbow."
At this, Seven looked up and said, "That's right, Five! Always lay the blame on others!"

"*You* can't talk!" said Five. "I heard the Queen say only yesterday you deserved to be punished!"

"What for?" said the one who'd spoken first.

"For bringing the cook tulip-roots instead of onions!"

Seven threw down his brush and began to say, "Well, of all the unjust things—", when he spotted Alice watching them, and stopped. The others looked around, too, and they bowed low.

"Would you tell me," said Alice rather timidly, "why you're painting those roses?"

Five and Seven said nothing but looked at Two, who began in a low voice, "Well Miss, this should have been a red rose tree but we put a white one in by mistake. If the Queen finds out, we'll all be punished."

At that moment Five, who'd been anxiously looking across the garden, called out "The Queen! The Queen!" and the three gardeners threw themselves flat upon their faces. Alice looked around to see a procession approaching.

First, there were ten soldiers carrying clubs—these were all shaped like the three gardeners, oblong and flat, with their hands and feet at the corners. Next came ten courtiers decorated with diamonds, walking in pairs like the soldiers. After this, ten royal children decorated with hearts and jumping merrily along in pairs. Next, the guests, mostly Kings and Queens, and then Alice spotted the White Rabbit, who was talking quickly and smiling in a nervous manner. Then, the Knave of Hearts, carrying the King's crown on a crimson velvet cushion. Last of all, came the King and Queen of Hearts.

 ## COLOR-CHANGING FLOWERS

There's more than one way to change a flower's color.

Turn to page 112 to transform a bunch of white carnations into a colorful bouquet!

WHAT COLORS DO YOU SEE?

The objects around you absorb and reflect light differently—this is what gives them their color.

A red rose reflects red light and a white rose reflects white light. Every color, other than the one that is reflected, is absorbed so we don't see them.

The colors that we do see depend on the wavelength of light detected by our eyes.

Lower frequencies (with longer wavelengths) are seen as red and orange, higher frequencies (with shorter wavelengths) are seen as violet and blue, and mid-range frequencies appear as green.

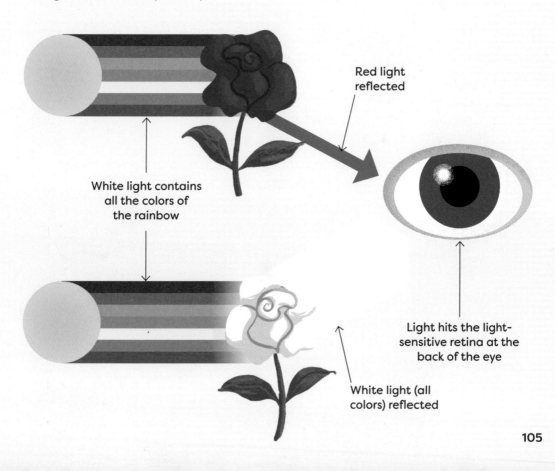

Red light reflected

White light contains all the colors of the rainbow

Light hits the light-sensitive retina at the back of the eye

White light (all colors) reflected

When the procession passed Alice, they all stopped and looked at her.
The Queen asked the Knave of Hearts severely, "Who's this?" and he
just bowed and smiled in reply.

"Idiot!" said the Queen, tossing her head impatiently, and turning
to Alice. "What's your name, child?"

"My name is Alice, if you please your Majesty," said Alice politely, but
she thought to herself, "Why, they're just a pack of cards! I needn't be
afraid of them."

"And who are *these*?" said the Queen, pointing to the three gardeners
lying by the rose tree. The pattern on their backs was the same as the
rest of the pack, so she couldn't tell anyone apart.

"How should *I* know?" said Alice, surprised by her own courage.

The Queen turned crimson with fury, and after glaring at her for
a moment, she screamed "Off with her head! Off—"

"Nonsense!" said Alice, very loudly and the Queen was silent.
She turned angrily away from her.

"Get up!" said the Queen, in a shrill, loud voice, and the three
gardeners jumped up, and began bowing to everyone present.

"Enough!" screamed the Queen. "You're making me giddy." Turning
to the rose tree, she went on, "What *have* you been doing here?"

PICKING COLORS

In art theory, the colors of the rainbow are contained within a color wheel (although our eyes can detect many more colors!).

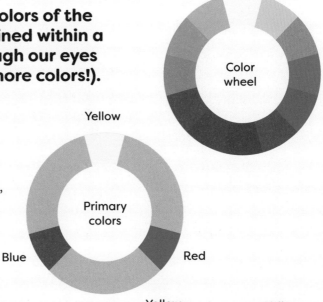

Color wheel

There are three primary colors, three secondary colors, and six tertiary colors. The primary colors, red, blue, and yellow, are used to create all other colors.

Primary colors

Yellow

Blue

Red

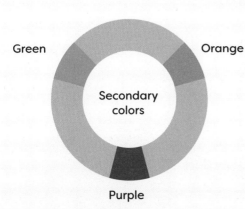

Green

Orange

Secondary colors

Purple

Secondary colors are made by mixing two primary colors together. They are purple, green, and orange.

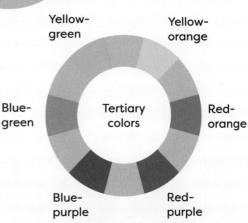

Yellow-green

Yellow-orange

Blue-green

Tertiary colors

Red-orange

Blue-purple

Red-purple

Tertiary colors are made by mixing a primary and secondary color together. On the color wheel, they are all the colors in between the primary and secondary colors.

"If you please, your Majesty," said Two, in a very humble voice, going down on one knee as he spoke, "we were trying—"

"I see!" said the Queen, who meanwhile had been examining the roses. "Off with their heads!" and the procession moved on.

The gardeners ran to Alice for protection. Three soldiers came past looking for them but soon gave up their search.

"Can you play croquet?" the Queen said. The soldiers were silent, and looked at Alice, as the question was obviously meant for her.

"Yes!" shouted Alice.

"Come on then!" roared the Queen, and Alice joined the procession.

"It's—it's a lovely day!" said a timid voice beside her. She was walking next to the White Rabbit, who was peeping anxiously into her face.

"Yes, lovely," said Alice, "—where's the Duchess?"

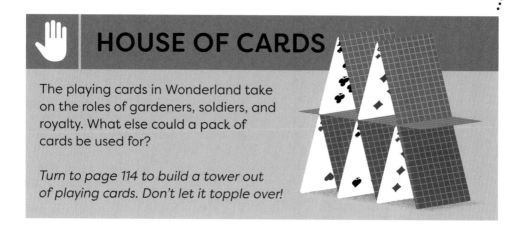

✋ HOUSE OF CARDS

The playing cards in Wonderland take on the roles of gardeners, soldiers, and royalty. What else could a pack of cards be used for?

Turn to page 114 to build a tower out of playing cards. Don't let it topple over!

"Hush! Hush!" said the Rabbit in a low, hurried voice. He looked anxiously over his shoulder as he spoke, and then raised himself up on tiptoes and whispered, "She's going to be punished."

"What for?" said Alice.

"Did you say 'What a pity!'?" the Rabbit asked.

"No, I didn't," said Alice. "I don't think it's a pity. I said 'What for?'"

"She boxed the Queen's—" the Rabbit began. Alice gave a little squeal of laughter. "Oh, hush!" the Rabbit whispered in a frightened tone. "The Queen will hear you! You see, she came rather late, and the Queen said—"

"Get to your places!" shouted the Queen with a voice of thunder. People began running about in all directions but once they'd settled, the game began. Alice thought she'd never seen such a curious croquet-ground in her life—it had little hills and dips, the balls were live hedgehogs, the mallets were flamingos, and the soldiers had to double themselves up to stand on their hands and feet, to make the arches.

The main difficulty for Alice was managing her flamingo. She could get his body tucked comfortably enough under her arm, with his legs hanging down, but just as she'd got his neck nicely straightened out and was going to give the hedgehog a blow with his head, he'd twist himself around and look up at her with such a puzzled expression she couldn't help bursting out with laughter.

When she got his head down, and was going to try again, she found that the hedgehog had unrolled itself, and was about to crawl away! On top of this, the soldiers were always getting up and walking off. It was a very difficult game indeed.

To make matters even worse, the players all played at once and fought for the hedgehogs. Before long, the Queen was furious and went stamping about shouting "Off with his head!" or "Off with her head!"

Alice began to feel uneasy. She was looking for a way to escape when she noticed a curious appearance in the air. After a minute or two, she recognized a grin and said to herself, "Why, it's the Cheshire Cat!"

"How are you getting on?" said the Cat, as soon as there was enough mouth for it to speak.

Alice waited until the eyes appeared, and then nodded. "It's no use

speaking to him," she thought, "until the ears have come, or at least one of them." When the whole head appeared, Alice put down her flamingo and began describing the croquet game.

"I don't think they play at all fairly," she complained, "and they all quarrel dreadfully—and they don't seem to have any particular rules, or at least, nobody follows them—and you've no idea how confusing it is, with everything being alive. I should have croqueted the Queen's hedgehog just now, but he ran away when he saw mine coming!"

"How do you like the Queen?" asked the Cat in a low voice.

"Not at all," said Alice, "she's so extremely—" Just then, she noticed the Queen was close behind her, listening, so she went on, "—likely to win, that it's hardly worthwhile finishing the game."

The Queen smiled and passed on.

"Who are you talking to?" said the King, approaching Alice, and looking at the Cat's head with curiosity.

"It's a friend of mine—a Cheshire Cat," said Alice.

"Well, he must be removed," said the King decisively, and he called the Queen. "My dear! I wish you would have this cat removed!"

The Queen had only one way of settling difficulties, great or small. "Off with his head!" she said, without even looking around.

The King looked pleased and hurried off to fetch a soldier.

MAKE COLOR-CHANGING FLOWERS

The Queen's gardeners are busy painting all the white roses red to please her Majesty. There's another way to change a flower's color and it takes no painting at all...

1
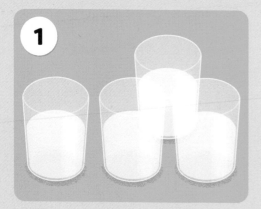

Half-fill each glass with water.

YOU WILL NEED:

- 4 glasses • Water
- Food coloring x4 colors
- 4 white carnations (or white flowers)
- Scissors • Paper
- Pen or pencil

2

Add 10-15 drops of food coloring to each glass, using a different color in each. Give the water a swirl to mix.

3

Trim the stems of your flowers so they can sit comfortably in the glasses of water.

TIP
You can try this experiment with as many different colors as you want. Different types of white flowers work well too.

4

Place one flower in each glass and leave them somewhere safe where they won't be knocked over!

5

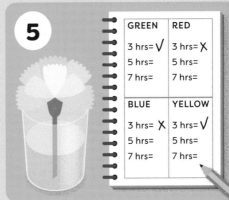

GREEN	RED
3 hrs= √	3 hrs= X
5 hrs=	5 hrs=
7 hrs=	7 hrs=

BLUE	YELLOW
3 hrs= X	3 hrs= √
5 hrs=	5 hrs=
7 hrs=	7 hrs=

Leave the flowers for 3 hours and then check on them. Can you see any color in the petals? Return every 2-3 hours to check progress. Use the paper to record your results each time.

6

Finally, leave the flowers overnight. What do they look like in the morning?

WHY IT WORKS

Usually, plants absorb water through their roots. The water travels up the stem and into the flower through small tubes called capillaries. In this case, the food coloring is pulled up the capillaries along with the water, giving the petals their color.

113

BUILD A HOUSE OF CARDS

Can you build a tower out of a pack of cards? You'll need a steady hand and some patience— how tall can you build it?

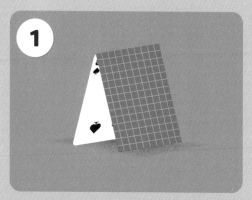

1

Choose a flat surface that has some grip (is not too slippery). Take two playing cards and lean them together to form an upside-down "V" shape.

YOU WILL NEED:
- Flat surface
- Pack of playing cards

TIP

Older cards that are less glossy are easier to build with because they have more friction (see page 13).

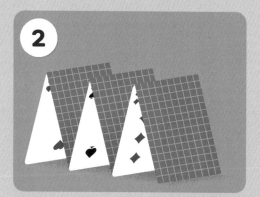

2

Repeat this process so you have three upside-down "V"s, or triangles, standing side by side, with a small gap between each triangle. This might take some practice!

3

Once the base of your tower looks secure, carefully place two playing cards horizontally on top of the three triangles, creating a platform.

4

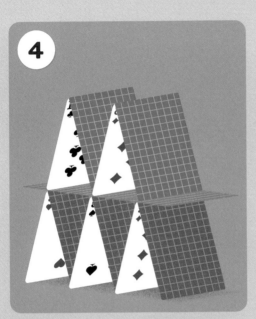

Balance another triangle on top of the platform. Each additional triangle should sit in the middle of the two triangles below it. Repeat on the other side.

5

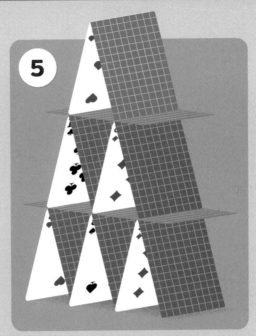

Place a card horizontally above this layer to create another platform. Then, carefully, balance a final triangle on top. Has it stayed upright?

6

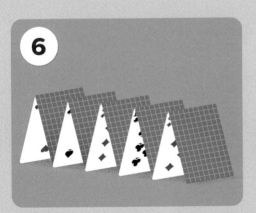

Experiment with making your tower taller by making the base wider.

WHY IT WORKS

The stability of your tower will rely on a number of factors. The most stable tower will be built on a flat surface with some friction (see page 13), the cards will be well-used, giving them some grip, and each triangle, or apex, will need to be matching in form. Plus, you'll need a steady hand!

Chapter 9

The Mock Turtle's Story

Alice could hear the Queen's voice in the distance, screaming with rage. She returned to the game, but her hedgehog was fighting with another hedgehog and her flamingo was on the other side of the garden, trying to fly up into a tree.

"Never mind," thought Alice, "all the arches are gone from this side of the ground anyway."

She went back to talk to the Cheshire Cat and found a large crowd had gathered around him. There was a dispute going on between a soldier, the King, and the Queen, while the rest looked uncomfortable.

When Alice appeared, they asked her how they should punish a cat who's only partially visible. The only thing Alice could think of to say was, "It belongs to the Duchess, you'd better ask *her*."

 ## MAKE AN ORIGAMI CAT

With his wide grin, the Cheshire Cat knows how to attract attention.

Turn to page 126 to make the floating head of the Cheshire Cat out of paper.

"She's in prison," said the Queen to the soldier, "fetch her here." And the soldier darted off like an arrow.

As soon as he'd gone, the Cat's head began fading away, and by the time the Duchess appeared, he'd disappeared completely.

"You can't imagine how glad I am to see you again, dear!" said the Duchess, as she tucked her arm affectionately into Alice's.

Alice was glad to find the Duchess in such a pleasant mood and wondered if the pepper had made her grumpy before. "Maybe it's pepper that makes people hot-tempered," she considered, pleased to have found a new kind of rule, "and vinegar that makes them sour—"

"You're thinking about something, my dear," the Duchess interjected, coming a little closer, "and that makes you forget to talk. I can't tell you what the moral of that is, but I shall remember in a bit."

"Perhaps it doesn't have one?" Alice suggested.

"Everything's got a moral," said the Duchess, "if only you can find it."

Alice didn't like being so close to the Duchess. Firstly, because she was *very* ugly, and secondly, because she was exactly the right height to rest her uncomfortably sharp chin on Alice's shoulder.

"The game's getting better now," Alice said, not wanting to be rude.

"It is," said the Duchess, "and the moral of that is: 'Oh, it's love, it's love, that makes the world go round!'"

INVISIBLE WORLDS

Our eyes are limited—we can't see everything that exists around us. Forces, atoms, and bacteria are some of the many things that make up the invisible world.

Everything is made up of atoms—including you. These tiny building blocks are far too small for your eyes (or even a really powerful microscope) to see. In fact, individual atoms are so small they're invisible to light waves, which travel straight past them.

A stack of 1,000,000 atoms would be about as thick as a sheet of paper.

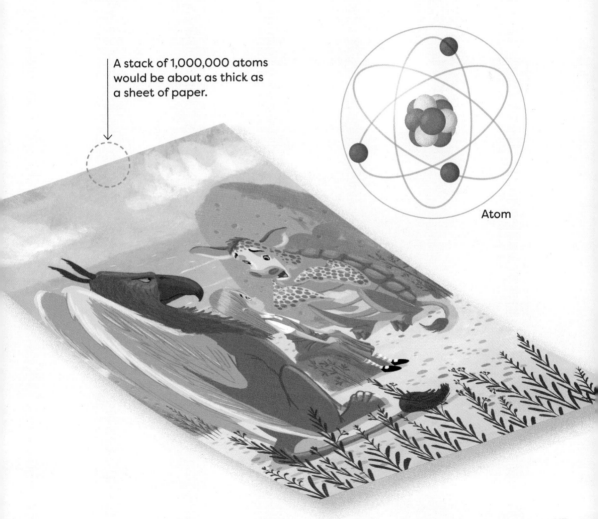

Atom

"How fond she is of finding morals in things!" Alice thought.

They kept walking. "Thinking again?" the Duchess asked, with another dig of her sharp little chin.

"I've a right to think," said Alice curtly.

"Just about as much right," said the Duchess, "as pigs have to fly; and the m—"

But to Alice's great surprise, the Duchess's voice died away and the arm linked with hers began to tremble. Alice looked up, and there stood the Queen with her arms folded, frowning like a thunderstorm.

"It's a lovely day, your Majesty!" the Duchess said meekly.

"Now, this is your last chance," shouted the Queen, stamping on the ground. "Either you leave, or you'll be punished. It's your choice!"

The Duchess was gone in an instant.

"Let's get on with the game," the Queen said to Alice. Alice was too frightened to speak, but slowly followed her all the same. The other guests, who had taken advantage of the Queen's absence and were resting in the shade, hurried back to the game.

The Queen continued shouting "Off with his head!" or "Off with her head!" Some players were taken into custody by the soldiers, who had to stop being arches for a time. After half an hour or so, all the players, except the King, the Queen, and Alice, were in custody.

Then the Queen stopped playing and said to Alice, "Have you seen the Mock Turtle yet?"

"No," said Alice. "I don't even know what a Mock Turtle is."

"It's the thing Mock Turtle Soup is made from," said the Queen.

"I've never seen one or heard of one," replied Alice.

"Come on, then," said the Queen, "he shall tell you his story."

As they walked off together, Alice heard the King say in a low voice to those present, "You're all pardoned."

Very soon, they came across a Gryphon lying asleep in the sun. "Up you get, lazy thing!" said the Queen, "and take this young lady to hear the Mock Turtle's story."

The Gryphon sat up and rubbed his eyes. He watched the Queen until she was out of sight, then chuckled. "What fun!" he said.

"What *is* the fun?" said Alice.

"Why, *she*," said the Gryphon. "It's all an illusion—she never punishes anyone, you know. Come on!"

They hadn't gone far when they saw the Mock Turtle in the distance. Alice could hear him sighing as if his heart would break. "Whatever makes him so sad?" she asked, and the Gryphon answered as before, "It's all an illusion—he hasn't got any sorrow, you know. Come on!"

As they approached, the Mock Turtle looked at them with large eyes full of tears.

"This young lady," began the Gryphon, "would like to hear your story."

"I'll let her," said the Mock Turtle sorrowfully. "Sit down, both of you, and don't speak a word until I've finished."

So they sat down, and nobody spoke for quite some time.

"Once," said the Mock Turtle at last, with a sigh, "I was a real Turtle."

There followed a very long silence, broken only by the occasional exclamation of "Hjckrrh!" from the Gryphon.

"When we were little," the Mock Turtle continued at last, "we went

✋ WRITE SECRET MESSAGES

Wonderland is full of weird and wonderful illusions.

Make invisible ink and use it to create your own magical illusion—turn to page 128.

to school in the sea. The master was an old Turtle—we used to call him Tortoise—"

"Why did you call him Tortoise, if he wasn't one?" Alice asked.

"We called him Tortoise because he *taught us*," said the Mock Turtle angrily. "Really, you're very dull!"

Poor Alice felt she wanted the ground to swallow her up.

"Yes, we had the best education. We learned Reeling and Writhing to begin with. Then the different branches of Arithmetic—Ambition, Distraction, Uglification, and Derision.

"I've never heard of 'Uglification,'" said Alice. "What's that?"

"You know what to beautify is, I suppose?" said the Gryphon.

"Yes," said Alice doubtfully, "it means to make something prettier."

"Well then," the Gryphon continued. "If you don't know what to uglify is, you're stupid."

Alice turned back to the Mock Turtle. "And how many hours a week did you do lessons?" she asked.

"Ten hours the first day," said the Mock Turtle. "Nine the next, and so on."

"How strange!" exclaimed Alice.

"That's the reason they're called lessons," the Gryphon remarked, "because they *lessen* from day to day."

"That's enough about lessons," the Gryphon interrupted, "tell her something about the games now."

"Perhaps you were never introduced to a lobster, so you'll have no idea what a Lobster Quadrille is!" The Mock Turtle began to demonstrate a type of dance with a little help from the Gryphon, while they sang.

"Thank you, that was wonderful!" Alice said, glad that it was all over.

"Now," said the Gryphon, "let's hear some of *your* adventures." Alice sat down and told them everything about her day. When she got to the part about her difficulty reciting verses, she felt exasperated.

"Shall we try the Lobster Quadrille again?" the Gryphon asked to lighten the mood. "Or the Mock Turtle could sing another song?"

"Oh, a song please," Alice replied eagerly. As the Mock Turtle sang, they heard a cry in the distance—"The trial's beginning!"

"Come on!" cried the Gryphon, taking Alice by the hand and hurrying off, without waiting for the song to end.

"What trial?" Alice panted as she ran, but the Gryphon only answered, "Come on!" and ran faster, while the sound of the Mock Turtle's song grew fainter in the breeze.

OPTICAL ILLUSIONS

Illusions trick us into thinking something looks different to how it exists in reality, so we might "see" something that isn't really there.

This is because the communication between your eyes and your brain gets mixed up and the brain gets confused by what your eyes are telling it!

Illusions might trick you into thinking that a still image is moving or make you see shapes and colors that aren't really there. What do you see here?

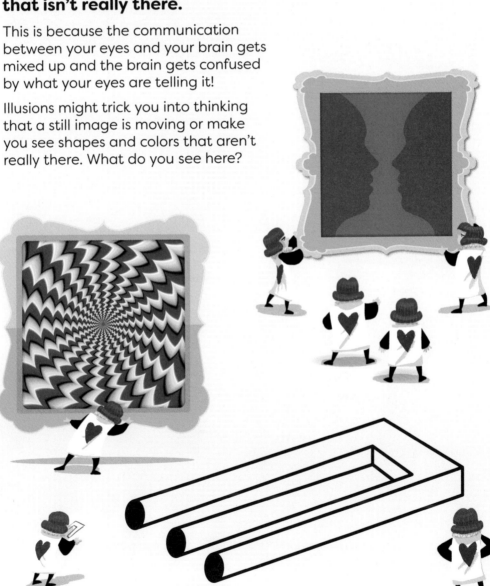

MAKE AN ORIGAMI CAT

Make the floating head of the Cheshire Cat out of paper.
Don't forget his dazzling ear-to-ear grin!

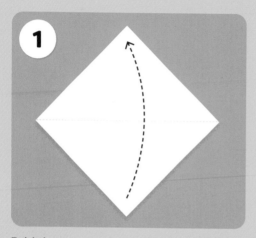

1

Fold the square of paper in half, bringing together two opposite corners to create a triangle.

YOU WILL NEED:

- Square piece of paper
- Colored chalks or markers
- Sticky tape (optional)

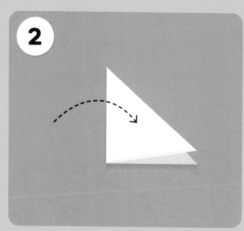

2

Fold your triangle in half again to make a smaller triangle, then unfold this last fold.

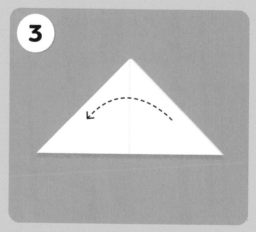

3

Lie the triangle flat on a table with its longest edge closest to you and the point facing away from you.

TIP

Once you've finished folding, you can use sticky tape to secure the folds at the back of the head if you want to.

4

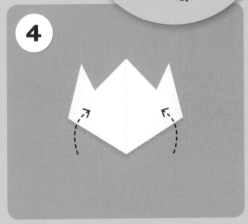

Fold the two corners closest to you (on the left and right) so that they point away from you, as shown.

5

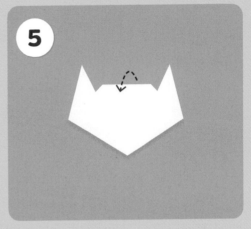

Fold a section of the top corner down to create a flat top. Turn the paper over.

6

Your paper should now look like the Cheshire Cat's head. Use your chalks or markers to draw the cat's eyes, nose, whiskers, and signature grin.

# WHY IT WORKS

Origami, the craft of folding paper to make art, is thought to have originated in Japan. Origami is traditionally made for ceremonies and special occasions and is also used to make beautiful works of art. The popularity of origami has spread across the world—there are countless patterns you can try.

SECRET MESSAGES

Keep top secret messages safe by writing them in invisible ink. Only those in the know will be able to reveal them!

1

Ask an adult to cut the lemon in half. Squeeze the juice into the bowl.

YOU WILL NEED:

- 1 lemon
- Small bowl
- Piece of paper
- Small paintbrush

2

Dip your paintbrush into the lemon juice and then use it to write your message on the piece of paper.

3

Keep topping up the lemon juice on your paintbrush as you write your message.

TIP
You can swap the lemon juice for an alternative acidic liquid, such as apple juice, vinegar, or milk.

4

Let your message dry.

5

With an adult's help, plug in a clothing iron and turn it up high. Glide it slowly over the piece of paper. Don't pause for too long on any one spot as your paper could burn.

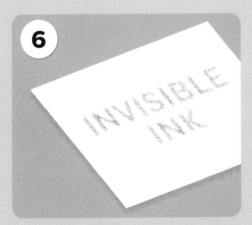

6

Carefully switch off the iron. Can you see your secret message becoming visible?

WHY IT WORKS

The lemon juice undergoes a chemical reaction (oxidization) under the heat of the iron. This turns the invisible juice on the paper a brown color, making it visible.

Chapter 10

Who Stole the Tarts?

A great crowd had assembled in the courtroom. The King and Queen of Hearts were seated on their thrones and the Knave stood before them, in chains. The White Rabbit stood near the King, with a trumpet in one hand and a scroll of parchment in the other. A large dish of tarts lay on a table and made Alice feel quite ravenous.

Alice had never been in a court of justice before. She'd read about them in books and was pleased to find she recognized a few things. "That's the judge," she said to herself, "with the great wig." The judge was the King, wearing a crown over his wig. "And that's the jury-box," thought Alice, "and those twelve creatures I suppose are the jurors."

The jurors were writing on slates. One had a squeaky pencil (it was Bill, the Lizard), and Alice took the opportunity to grab it quickly!

The White Rabbit blew three blasts on the trumpet, unrolled the parchment scroll, and read out the accusation:

"The Queen of Hearts, she made some tarts, all on a summer day.
The Knave of Hearts, he stole those tarts, and took them quite away."

"Consider your verdict," the King said to the jury.

"Not yet!" the Rabbit interrupted hastily. "There's a lot to do first."

"Call the first witness," said the King, and the White Rabbit blew three blasts on the trumpet.

The first witness was the Hatter, who came in with a teacup in one hand and a piece of bread-and-butter in the other.

"Take off your hat," the King said to the Hatter.

"It isn't mine," the Hatter replied.

"Stolen!" the King exclaimed, turning to the jury.

"I keep them to sell," the Hatter explained. "I'm a hatter."

The Queen put on her spectacles and began staring at the Hatter, who turned pale.

"Give your evidence," said the King, "and don't be nervous, or we'll have to punish you too."

The Hatter kept shifting from one foot to the other, looking uneasy.

Just at that moment, Alice felt a curious sensation. She realized she was growing larger again!

The Queen was still staring at the Hatter. "Bring me the list of singers in the last concert!" she said to one of the officers of the court. At this, the poor Hatter trembled so much that he shook both his shoes off.

"Give your evidence," the King repeated angrily.

WHAT'S THAT SOUND?

The sound of the White Rabbit's trumpet bounces around the courtroom. How is the sound made and how does it travel?

When the White Rabbit blows into the trumpet, the air particles inside the instrument start to vibrate.

These vibrating particles make up sound waves, which transfer the sound from its source (the trumpet) to its surroundings (the courtroom).

When sound waves travel to your ear, they cause your eardrum to vibrate. The bigger the vibrations, the louder the sound.

Sound detected by eardrum

The bigger the sound wave, the louder the sound

Sound waves

Air particles vibrate

The Hatter described how he'd taken his tea and bread-and-butter, and began to explain what the March Hare and the Dormouse had said, but was trembling so much, he wasn't making much sense. Eventually, he went down on one knee. "I'm a poor man, your Majesty," he began. "You're a *very* poor *speaker*," the King replied.

"If that's all you know, you may stand down," continued the King.

The Hatter hurriedly left the court, without even putting his shoes on.

"Call the next witness!" said the King.

This time it was the turn of the Duchess's cook. She carried the pepper-box with her, making all the people by the door sneeze.

"Give your evidence!" said the King.

"Shan't," said the cook.

"What are tarts made of?" the King asked.

"Pepper, mostly," the cook replied.

"Treacle," said a sleepy voice behind her.

"Take that Dormouse away!" the Queen shrieked. "Off with his whiskers!"

For some minutes, the whole court was in confusion as the Dormouse was taken out. By the time they'd settled again, the cook had disappeared.

"Never mind!" said the King, with a sense of relief. "Call the next witness!"

The White Rabbit fumbled through his list, and to Alice's great surprise, his shrill, little voice said "Alice!"

"Here!" cried Alice, quite forgetting how large she'd grown. She jumped up in such a hurry, she tipped over the jury-box with her skirt, upsetting all the jurors onto the heads of the crowd below.

"I'm terribly sorry!" Alice exclaimed, and began picking them up.

"The trial cannot proceed," said the King in a grave voice, "until all the jurors are in their places," looking hard at Alice as he said so.

Alice looked at the jury-box and saw that in her haste she'd put Bill head downward. The poor little thing was waving his tail about, quite unable to move. She soon put him right.

MAKE A NEWTON'S CRADLE

Alice knocks the jury-box with great force causing the jurors to collide with each other.

Build a Newton's Cradle on page 140 to see these forces in action.

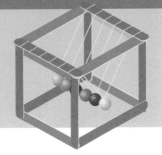

As soon as the jury had regained their composure, they continued.

"What do you know about this business?" the King said to Alice.

"Nothing whatever," said Alice.

"That's very important," said the King, turning to the jury.

"*Un*important, your Majesty means, of course," the White Rabbit interjected.

"Of course," said the King. Then "Silence!" as he read out from his book, "Rule 42. *All persons more than a mile high to leave the court.*"

Everybody looked at Alice.

"*I'm* not a mile high," Alice said.

"You are," said the King. "Nearly two miles high," added the Queen.

"Well, I shan't leave," said Alice indignantly, "besides, you've just made that up!"

✋ HOW TALL IS ALICE?

Alice is towering over the jury, but no one can decide quite how tall she is.

To find out how to measure giant buildings (or very tall people), turn to page 142.

"It's the oldest rule in the book," said the King, and turning to the jury, said "Consider your verdict."

"There's more evidence to come," said the White Rabbit, jumping up. "This paper has just been picked up. It seems to be a letter, written by the Knave to—Oh, it doesn't say." He unfolded the paper. "Actually, it isn't a letter, it's a set of verses."

"Are they in the Knave's handwriting?" asked one of the jurymen.

"No," said the White Rabbit. The jury all looked puzzled.

"He must have disguised his writing," said the King.

"Please your Majesty," said the Knave. "I didn't write it, and they can't prove I did—there's no signed name at the end."

"If you didn't sign it," said the King, "you *must* have meant mischief. Only an honest man signs his name."

"That proves his guilt!" said the Queen.

"It proves nothing of the sort!" cried Alice, who'd grown so large in the last few minutes, she wasn't at all afraid of interrupting the King.

They discussed the verses for some time but got nowhere. "Let the jury consider their verdict!" the King cried again.

"No!" said the Queen. "Sentence first—verdict afterward."

"That's the most absurd thing I've ever heard," cried Alice.

"Off with her head!" the Queen shouted at the top of her voice.

"Who cares anyway," Alice cried, who was now her full size, "you're nothing but a pack of cards!"

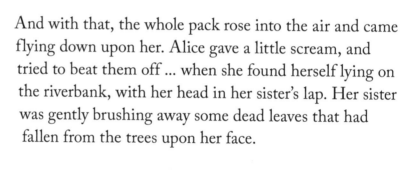

And with that, the whole pack rose into the air and came flying down upon her. Alice gave a little scream, and tried to beat them off ... when she found herself lying on the riverbank, with her head in her sister's lap. Her sister was gently brushing away some dead leaves that had fallen from the trees upon her face.

"Oh, I've had the strangest dream," said Alice, and she told her sister all about her adventures.

At tea time, Alice ran off, thinking what a wonderful dream it had been, while her sister stayed, watching the sunset. She imagined the White Rabbit, the rattle of teacups and the shrill voice of the Queen. Then she pictured how her little sister would one day be grown up, and perhaps tell her own children about Wonderland, remembering their happy summer days.

THE END

LOOK CLOSER...

Magnifying glasses and eyeglasses help people to see small details more clearly—which is vital when studying evidence in court.

Both devices use a lens to make an image appear larger or sharper.

A magnifying glass has a convex lens, which is thicker in the middle than it is at the edges.

A convex lens refracts (bends) light rays, causing them to converge (come together) at a single point called the focal point.

This creates a "virtual image" that looks bigger than the real image, allowing small details to be seen.

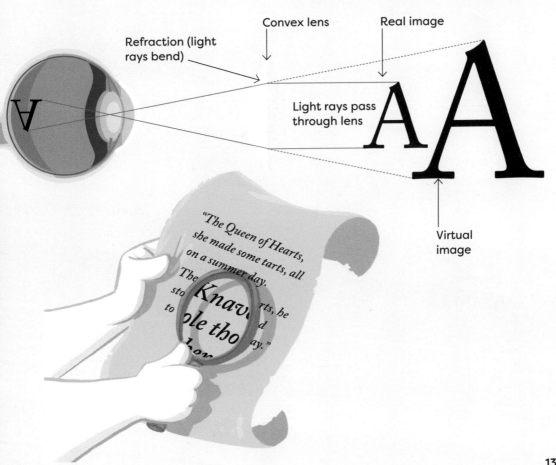

Convex lens

Real image

Refraction (light rays bend)

Light rays pass through lens

Virtual image

"The Queen of Hearts, she made some tarts, all on a summer day.
The Knave sto... rts, he ... to ... ole tho... ay."

MAKE A NEWTON'S CRADLE

As Alice jumps up to take her place in court, she knocks over the jury-box, sending the jurors flying. This is momentum in action—the force of an object as it moves. Momentum also makes this Newton's Cradle work.

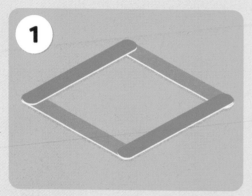

1

With an adult's help, glue 4 craft sticks together to make a square. Do the same with 4 more craft sticks and allow them to dry. This is your frame.

YOU WILL NEED:

- 14 craft sticks or ice pop sticks
- Hot glue gun/ strong glue
- String
- Scissors
- Pencil
- 6 marbles
- Ruler
- Tape

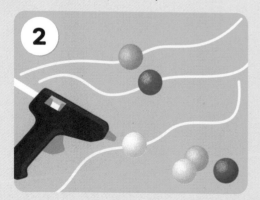

2

Cut 6 pieces of string that are 8 in (20 cm) long. With an adult's help, carefully glue gun one marble at the center of each piece of string.

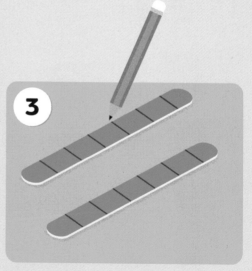

3

On another craft stick, make 6 marks that are each 0.6 in (1.5 cm) apart. Repeat with a second craft stick.

4

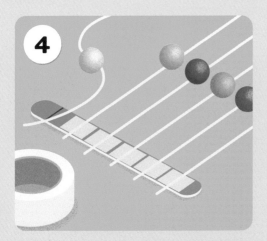

Tape one end of each marble string to the marked craft stick so that the strings line up with the marks.

5

To construct the frame, stand your craft stick squares (from step 1) so they face each other. Use the hot glue gun to join each of the opposite corners with a craft stick. This will create a cube.

6

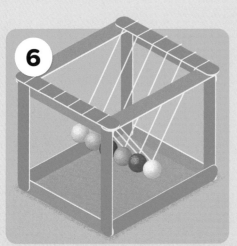

Glue the marked craft stick from step 4 to one side of the top of the frame. Place the second marked craft stick opposite it and tape the marble strings into place so they line up with the marks.

Make sure the marbles all line up with each other when viewed from above and the side. Lift and release a marble at one end and see what happens!

WHY IT WORKS

Momentum is the force of an object as it moves. When you swing a marble at one end, it hits the one next to it and the force travels through each marble until it reaches the other end, pushing the last marble upward. When that marble swings back down, the force of the collision with the marble next to it passes through the marbles again.

EXTREME MEASUREMENTS

To find out how tall Alice—or any other tall object— is, all you need is a long pole or stick, a measuring tape, and some sunshine. Give this a try!

1 Choose the subject whose height you want to measure. Then find a nearby open space to carry out your experiment. The space in between you and your subject will need to be free of obstacles.

YOU WILL NEED:

- Long pole or broom stick
- Measuring tape
- Sunny day
- Pencil • Paper

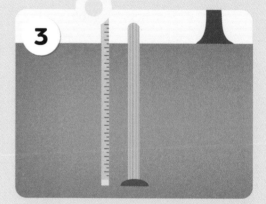

2 Find a way to stand your pole so that it points straight upward, for example, by pushing it into the ground if you're on soil.

3 Measure the length of your pole from top to bottom (just the section that is above ground) and write this down.

4

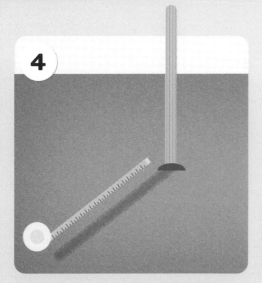

Now for a bit of patience. Keep an eye on the pole's shadow as the Sun moves across the sky. When the length of the pole's shadow is equal to the height of the pole, you'll need to act fast.

5

Once the length of the pole and its shadow are equal, take your measuring tape to the base of your subject.

6

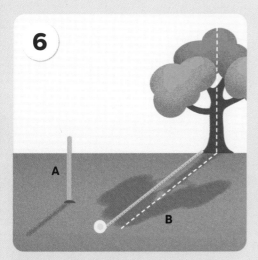

Measure the length of the subject's shadow, from the base to the tip of the shadow. This measurement will be equal to its height!

WHY IT WORKS

When the pole's height and its shadow (A) are equal in length, the subject's shadow (B) and its unknown height will also be equal in length. This is because both objects stand at 90-degree angles to the ground, forming right-angled triangles. You can remember it like this:

When known height = shadow length A, unknown height = shadow length B.